FIRST
AID
FR
JEWISH
MARRIAGES

RABBI DANIEL SCHONBUCH, M/

ISBN: 1-4392-3266-0
EAN13: 9781439232668

Visit Rabbi Daniel Schonbuch online at
www.neverbeyondreach.org or email him at
rabbischonbuch@yahoo.com.

Visit www.booksurge.com to order additional copies.

Dedicated to the memory of Rabbi Gavriel and
Rivkah Holtzberg H"YD

TABLE OF CONTENTS

ACKNOWLEDGEMENTS

I would like to acknowledge my wife Daniella, the most important person in my life, for making this book possible. Through her own personal achievements and love for me and our children, she has led the way in building a wonderful and fulfilling marriage. She embodies many of the principles that are the foundation of this book. From the first page to the last, her dedication to allowing me the late nights needed to write this book and her support in making sure I finally finished this work, made it all possible.

A special thanks to Rabbi Kadish Waldman of Jerusalem, who has shown me tremendous insight into the inner dynamics of marriage and the spiritual possibilities that a Jewish family can achieve.

CHAPTER 1
FIRST AID FOR YOUR MARRIAGE

In This Chapter:

- Emotional First Aid For Your Marriage
- Why Most Marriages Can Work
- Focus on Your Relationship

Are you looking for emotional first aid for your marriage? If you are, you're not alone. Engaged couples, newlyweds and those who have been married for years, are looking for ways to make their marriages better or to simply heal their emotional wounds.

As a therapist, I know that there are so many relationship problems that could be resolved if people had an emotional GPS that could guide them through marriage. Others could use a bit of emotional first aid that can give them immediate results and help them buy time to work out the inner dynamics of their marriage before they draw their own conclusions. Often couples just need a small amount of reassurance that their problems will work out - and with some guidance – that their marriage will get better.

I'm also not surprised that people are feeling insecure about the state of marriages in America. It's almost impossible to turn on the radio or read a website that doesn't have negative information about marriage today. Take the latest studies on divorce. A recent study called "The Effects of Divorce In America" showed a significant increase in divorce over the last seven decades. The report found that:

"In 1935, there were 16 divorces for each 100 marriages. By 1998, the number had risen to 51 divorces per 100 marriages." In addition, "over a twenty year period the number of divorced Americans rose from 4.3 million in 1970 to 18.3 million in 1996."

The statistics speak for themselves: relationships in America are in trouble and as a society we are experiencing more divorce and dysfunction than ever before.

It is true that the Torah community does not share these

same statistics; our marriages tend to last longer and the viability of Jewish marriage is one of the great examples of the power and the wisdom of the Torah. However, over the last few years, we are beginning to see a new trend. Not a month will pass by when we don't hear about a young couple getting divorced. The fact is, thirty years ago, "divorce" was an almost unspoken word in the Torah community. Today, divorce is becoming more common and we may be viewing the beginning of a new and dangerous trend. As a case in point, a colleague of mine recently mentioned to me that he stopped giving engagement gifts and preferred to wait until the couple took the final steps to the chupah! These are signs that relationships are becoming harder to solidify and more difficult to maintain.

I have also witnessed that young adults looking to get married are becoming wary of promises that, "things will just work out," and "love will conquer all." Many are willing to try just about anything to know for certain whether their marriage will succeed. In fact, some are so desperate for iron-clad assurances about their relationships, that they are willing to spend hours searching online for articles on marriage, participating in forums, and even taking illusive five-minute quizzes that promise to see if they have found their "true love."

Here's an ad I saw for one such dubious website: "Doubting if the person you are with is the right one for you? These tests and quizzes will help you to disclose his or her true essence."

And that was just one site. There are so many others online that promise answers about romantic compatibility, how to know if you have found your soul mates, how much you have in common, and whether your love will last forever. It's easy to get sucked into the appealing veneer of these quick and easy answers that aren't based on fact or sound judgment.

I believe that most marriages can work. As I said earlier, often all they need is a little guidance and direction, and when necessary, a bit of emotional first aid.

Take Yossi, 25, and Deborah, 22, a young couple that came to talk with me about their fears of marriage and their inability to build a meaningful relationship. When they first walked into my office I was struck by how well they appeared – at least on the outside. They were in the prime of their lives, well dressed, soft spoken and well educated. Yossi was a systems analyst for a software company, and Deborah was a graduate student who had just started her first year in a master's degree program in psychology.

Yossi, it turned out, was having difficulty in deciding whether or not to get married. Deborah was scared that he couldn't make up his mind and that he was unable to commit to a stable relationship. Yossi had other concerns about marrying Deborah. He was uneasy about the negative vibes he was receiving from what he described as Deborah's "well-to-do" family. He was sensing that they would be unwilling to support them while Deborah was still in graduate school, and he was worried that he couldn't carry the financial burden alone.

They were both unsure of their future and didn't know if this was going to be a successful marriage. Like other young couples, they wanted to know if there was some kind of crystal ball that I could gaze into to tell them if their marriage would work. I told them that I wasn't a magician, but I could offer them some sound advice about relationships. I explained that the key to marriage was something that has been known from time immemorial. In fact, it is so simple and profound that most couples (barring serious emotional illness or domestic abuse) could utilize it to greatly enhance their chances of staying happily married.

No doubt, Yossi and Deborah would be challenged by financial concerns, work stress, childrearing, and difficult in-law relationships. Amidst the ups and downs of everything waiting for them — happy and disappointing moments, quality times enjoyed together and stressful late nights at work, watching their children take their first steps and struggling at school— the "secret," that could hold their marriage together and bring them the most happiness and stability in their lives, would be to focus on the primal importance of their relationship.

I call this simple yet revolutionary idea Relationship Theory, which states that for a marriage to work, both husband and wife need to make their relationship the main goal of their lives.

Another way of stating this is:
$$H = QR$$

Where, Happiness (H) is directly proportional to the Quality of Relationship (QR) one develops with their spouse. The more that a couple works on deepening both the quality and quantity of their relationship, the greater likelihood they have for success.

A quality relationship allows two people to feel that they are appreciated by one another; that someone else exists in their lives that will listen to their pain without being judgmental; that there is someone that they can rely upon in times of need; that life doesn't have to be lived alone, but in company with someone who loves and cares about them.

Above all, a good relationship allows a person to bond with

another human being and experience the benefits of emotional closeness and companionship.

The idea of focusing on the relationship is not just a theory; it has been shown to increase the chances of marital stability and longevity.

A survey conducted in 2002, asked 135 couples who were married for over seven years or more to rate the level of happiness in their marriages where "1" would signify discontent and "5" would reflect a high level of satisfaction.

87% of the 107 couples who answered "3" or above (which connoted a relatively high level of marital satisfaction) stated that at the center of their marriage was a total commitment to their relationship.

Participants were also asked to comment on the key elements of their successful relationships. Here are some of their answers:

"We care about each other more than ourselves."

"My wife and I understand what each other needs."

"He is always there for me - and I'm there for him - no matter what we are going through."

"We put our relationship above everything else."

"My wife has a keen understanding of what makes me happy. I would do anything for her - and she knows how much I want her to be happy."

What was the key to their success? Overall they were committed to maintaining and strengthening their relationship. If, for example, anything came between them and put stress on their marriage they were able to reorient themselves back to each other and focus on the importance of their relationship.

The idea of focusing on the relationship is also based upon Torah principles. A relationship-centered marriage is alluded to at least seven times in *Shir HaShirim, The Song of Songs*. By studying these terms we see how the Torah describes a complete love relationship. The seven terms are: 1. *kalosi* - my bride; 2. *achosi* - my sister; 3. *rayosi* - my friend; 4. *yonosi* – my dove; 5. *tomosi* - my perfection; 6. *yafosi* - my beauty; 7. *dodi* - my beloved.

"My bride" clearly connotes the romantic, physical and male-female "role" aspects that are basic to marriage.

"My sister" connotes a close, deep familial bond that is free from the confusion that may arise out of the emotions of the romantic level. The bond is that of your flesh and blood. It provides the unconditional, non-physical and constant element of love-relationship that a romantic-only relationship lacks, which the family relationship has.

"My friend" implies that a spouse should first and foremost be viewed as a friend. We know that with friends we strive to treat them in a kind manner and are always careful to avoid insulting them or belittling them in any way. We also maintain a healthy amount of respect and never overstep boundaries. Of course there are different dimensions of marriage that go far beyond friendship, but friendship enables a deeper and more intimate relationship to emerge.

"My dove" - the dove is a member of the animal kingdom that chooses one mate and remains loyal to it for a lifetime. Use of the term "dove" in Shir HaShirim teaches that a spouse is for staying with for a life time - with this same person, with each loyal to the other. The Midrash says that the dove turns its head to look back at its nest longingly when it flies away from the nest. This teaches us that the dove knows that its support, its strength and the center of its life is the nest that it shares with its mate. Likewise, one's home and mate are the support, strength and center of one's life.

"My perfection." We know no one who is pure and faultless. Be we can accept our spouse and be satisfied as if the person is pure and perfect; by accepting faults, hang-ups, shortcomings, quirks and habits; and by appreciating wholeheartedly the qualities, attributes and strengths that make your mate special, precious, beautiful and unique. This is as if to say, "With all your faults, I love you no less than if you would be perfect."

"My beauty." One must be attracted to one's mate. Your mate should be one or more of: beautiful, handsome, adorable, pretty, pleasant, cute, appealing, attractive...in your eyes.

"My beloved." There must me endearment for there to be a bond. Your mate should be heartwarming to you. Through endearment, the couple has the love and affection that brings them to true oneness for a lifetime. The essence of building this is through both giving for the good and happiness of the other.

Out of all these levels alluded to in the Torah, I believe that focusing on "rayosi" or friendship is the first line of emotional first aid and healing.

That's why when couples like Yossi and Deborah come to speak with me about their fears of marriage, I suggest that they begin by asking themselves if they are willing to make their relationship a priority in their lives. If they don't, it's going to be very difficult, if not impossible, for them to succeed.

Relationship Quiz

So if you are looking for emotional first aid, start by asking yourself the following questions:

What are the most important principles of your marriage?

What where the dreams and aspirations that started your relationship?

Did you marry for comfort, pleasure, money or honor?

Are you willing to make your relationship the most important part of your marriage?

Visualizing your values and seeing whether or not they are central to your marriage can help you understand the road you are traveling on. Unfortunately, our society has sold us a distorted image of marriage, which maintains that external factors such as money or comfort are the factors that make marriage work. Just think about how popular culture depicts the perfect couple, who have all the conveniences one could ever imagine. They have all the money, pleasure, and fun they could ever want, but are they happy? That's the million dollar question.

Although some people may choose core values such as wealth, pleasure and honor for their marriage, in the long run, experience has shown that these external values are temporal. Happiness in life has very little to do with externals, and those who focus on the external values often find their relationships unsettled, lacking direction, and without the strength to last a lifetime. In fact, over the years, I have witnessed many families who have little financial means, yet have the power of a healthy relationship. Against the conventional wisdom that money alone buys happiness, these families prove that success is dependent on other variables such as spiritual values, healthy attitudes, and high levels of emotional intelligence. Above all, they are dedicated to maintaining and nurturing the most important commodity in their lives, their relationship.

Enter Into The Relationship Circle

That's why my advice to couples seeking to live their marriage beyond the moment is to place their relationship at the middle of the circle.

Take Mordechai, 36, and Chani, 35, who were married for six months and came to ask me for advice on how to save their relationship. They seemed to have everything going for them. They were working professionals, successful and upwardly mobile; they shared many common factors including similar religious beliefs, intelligence levels, and were both pleasantly extroverted.

Yet, soon after marriage, it was apparent that Mordechai and Chani didn't get along very well. Little things like the cleanliness of the house, or who made dinner, became mountain-sized issues that were often blown out of proportion. The quality of their relationship was going downhill and their marriage was in crisis. Only six months had passed since their chuppah and they were beginning to feel that they were unequipped to deal with each other's emotional needs. Instead, they tended to withdraw from one another and were avoiding taking the obvious step of working together to solve their issues.

On the outside, they seemed to have everything going for them, yet now they had little to show for it. What was causing their marital stress? Did they share some deeply-rooted negative patterns? Was it a question of personality differences? Did they have trouble managing their anger?

Before I offered them some emotional first aid, I asked them to draw an imaginary circle in the middle of the room, to represent their relationship. I then asked them to take their chairs and sit in the middle of the circle if they were committed to their relationship. My feeling was that if they weren't able to sit in the circle together, then their marriage would have little chance of succeeding.

I also made it clear to them that, statistically, the overwhelming majority of failed marriages (between two emotionally healthy individuals) end because couples are having trouble building and staying committed to their overall relationship.

A 1995 statewide survey in Utah, for example, examining why marriages end in divorce, found that the lack of commitment to the relationship was the top reason for the growing phenomenon.

Specifically, the Utah Marriage Survey asked Utahns who had been divorced to answer the following: "There are many reasons why marriages fail. I'm going to read a list of possible reasons. Looking back at your most recent divorce, tell me whether or not each factor was a major contributor to your divorce. You can say, 'yes,' or 'no,' to each factor."

The following responses show the percentages of those respondents who answered, "yes," to each factor that they felt was a major contributor to their divorce:

Men/Women/The Mean

Lack of commitment: 87%/79%/83%
Too much conflict and arguing: 48%/58%/53%
Infidelity or extramarital affairs: 47%/56%/52%
Getting married too young: 39%/43%/41%
Financial problems or economic hardship: 31%/35%/33%
Lack of support from family members: 21%/20%/21%
Little or no helpful premarital education: 19%/29%/24%
Other: 17%/28%/22%
Religious differences between partners: 13%/16%/15%
Domestic violence: 6%/37%/22%

The findings of the survey revealed what Utahns who have experienced divorce perceive: that the lack of commitment was the number one contributing factor to their divorces. Commitment often involves making one's partner and relationship a priority, investing in the marriage, and having a long-term view of the relationship.

Couples like Mordechai and Chani are a perfect example of a relationship that had migrated onto the back burner. And, as I predicted, after several weeks of counseling, it became apparent that there was nothing fundamentally wrong with this young couple. Neither was particularly high on "control". Neither of them had a history of serious emotional illness. And both came from parents who were happily married.

Mordechai and Chani needed to learn more about how to negotiate their emotions, how to communicate in a more effective way, and how to begin to recommit to their relationship.

First Aid Relationship Tips

If you're concerned about your relationship, you need to ask yourself the following questions:

- Do you view building the relationship a central principle of your marriage?

- Do you set aside time each day to nurture your relationship?

- Do you look for the good qualities in your spouse?

- Do you appreciate the small, kind acts your spouse does for you on a daily basis?

- Do you spend time thinking about the good moments, and limit time and energy spent focusing on the bad ones?

Most couples who evaluate their relationship find that the biggest hole in their marriage is the fact that they don't spend time and effort building their relationship. They allowed themselves to become complacent. Complacency in marriage allows emotional weeds to grow out of control. It catches and it spreads, silently and invisibly, and by the time you realize what is happening, much damage has been done.

It is so easy to fall into a daily routine, fueled by responsibilities, so that people forget what relationships are all about. With so much to do each day, and without the need to plan to tune into each other, relationships tend to be pushed to the back, treated as something that doesn't need to be attended to, and left to just bumble along. Often we fail to make time for our spouses. Or when we do, it often merely consists of stolen moments at the end of a long, hard day, when we lack the energy to show how much we truly love and appreciate each other, and we are just too tired to have any fun.

When spouses begin to feel neglected, they often start by making a subtle plea — a gentle reminder that they feel they aren't important any more, and that they feel unloved and undervalued.

Yet, all it takes is those small gestures — nothing fancy — just small and thoughtful little gestures that show love, respect and affection for each other. Such gestures are an indication that a husband or wife still appreciates their marriage, their relationship, and the life they have together.

Compliments should be regular: not a thing of the past or of just occasional mention, and not something that you believe is no longer required. Make sure your spouse knows that you appreciate them, respect them, love them and admire them, and above all, make sure that they know that you want to be with them forever.

Couples like Yossi and Devorah and Mordechai and Chani, took steps to change the direction of their marriage. They were willing to get into the "Relationship Circle" and create a new future together.

If you are like one of the 87% of the participants in the Utah survey who felt that their marriage was off course due to the lack of commitment to their relationship, or you simply need advice on how to reduce conflict and manage your differences more effectively, you now have a choice. The process begins by implementing the eight key steps that you will learn about in this book:

1. Enter into the Relationship Circle
2. Explore your inner worlds
3. Become an active listener
4. Reduce controlling behavior
5. Resolve conflict peacefully
6. Make a positive impact on your children
7. Manage your money wisely
8. Improve the relationship with your in laws

In the following chapters we will explore practical ways to increase your awareness of your spouse's inner world, build emotional equity, and create a relationship that will last a lifetime.

First Aid Relationship Tips

Focus on your relationship

Become your spouse's best friend

Compliment one another

First Aid Exercise 1: Relationship Renewal

---

1) What have you and your spouse done recently for renewal of your relationship?

2) What do you think your spouse would like to do for renewal (soon or in the next year)?

3) What would you like to do (soon or in the next year)?

4) How often do you REALLY just talk as a couple?

5) Why are you in this relationship in the first place?

6) What can you do as a couple to bring you closer together?

CHAPTER 2
THE ROAD MAP TO A HAPPY MARRIAGE: CONNECTING TO YOUR SPOUSE

In This Chapter:

• Connecting to Your Spouse's Inner World

• Five Levels of the Inner World

• Relationship Tests

• Emphasizing affirmation and mutual self esteem

Finding direction in marriage is similar to going on a long journey. To get to where you want to go, you will need to have a plan that includes directions, supplies and someone to navigate along the way. You will also have to be prepared for many possible factors that may interfere with your trip, including wind, rain, unpredictable mechanical breakdown and human error. Most importantly you will need a map to guide you on where to go and how to reorient yourself when you get off track.

Many couples who seek my advice are simply lacking the guidance of a relationship road map that could make a significant difference in their marriage.

Take Shmuel, 25 and Rivky, 23, who came to discuss the lack of excitement and enthusiasm in their marriage. They were only married for about six months, but were already feeling that after their smooth walk to the chupah, they were now traveling down a bumpy road to an unknown destination.

From the outset they looked like the perfect couple, well-dressed, articulate and extremely well-educated. All of the excitement surrounding their engagement period and wedding had just about ended. Now, in their sixth month of marriage, they began to feel that they were unequipped to deal with each other's emotional needs. They were constantly bickering about small things like garbage collection, cooking dinner and cleaning up around the house.

Marriage wasn't supposed to be so hard. Unable to cope, they started to withdraw from one another, instead of working together to solve their problems. It's important to note that these were two healthy individuals who had the potential to have a great marriage, but they were lacking a guidebook or emotional GPS that could guide them on how to communicate and gain greater understanding of one another.

This couple's relationship was clearly going off course. They needed guidance to stay focused on their destination.

To make their job easier, I suggested that they follow an emotional road map based upon what I call The Four Cs of Relationship Theory: Connection, Control, Communication, and Conflict Resolution. Together, the Four Cs of Relationship Theory provide a road map to help couples evaluate where the relationship is going, and where and how to make changes if necessary.

Imagine, for example if Shmuel and Rivky could read each other's minds and understand what makes them happy or sad; what they are scared about and ways that they like to be cared about.

The Four Cs help couples see the bigger picture, and then make a distinction between the areas that demand attention, and those other matters that are superficial and should not be the focus of their relationship. For example, you may find yourself arguing over small things like cleaning the dishes or doing the laundry. You may also start feeling that your spouse is overly controlling and denies your feelings. Or, you may feel that you are drifting apart and don't feel as connected as you used to. If so, the question becomes: should you try to be more assertive? Or should you learn more about you spouse's inner world, increase the amount of quality time you spend together, and carefully work through their issues with them? A look at the Four Cs should provide an answer. In this and the following chapters, you will learn how to put these principles into action.

Let's begin with the first "C" and learn how to connect to your spouse's inner world. As a therapist, I help couples explore both sides of their personalities; their external behavioral characteristics as well as their inner emotional worlds.

The process begins when we realize that all human beings live in two distinct emotional worlds: an outer world and an inner world. The outer world is merely a façade, an outer layer which covers up our deeper and unseen emotions. The inner world, however, is the place that holds the key to understanding what makes people tick.

How in touch are you with your spouse's inner world? Listed below are common negative behaviors that are based upon underlying "inner" world emotions. Take a few moments to evaluate your awareness of these issues.

Negative behavior: threats, attacks, sarcasm, rudeness —
How do you perceive your spouse's behavior?
What are their inner feelings?

Negative behavior: defensiveness, shyness, withdrawn, uncommunicative —
How do you perceive your spouse's behavior?
What are their inner feelings?

Negative behavior: judging, criticizing, disapproving —
How do you perceive your spouse's behavior?
What are their inner feelings?

Here are some possible answers:

Negative behavior: threats, attacks, sarcasm, rudeness —
How do you perceive your spouse's behavior? Obnoxious, hostile, aggressive
What are their inner feelings? Hurt, anxious, embarrassed, fearful

Negative behavior: defensiveness, shyness, withdrawn, uncommunicative —
How do you perceive your spouse's behavior? Rejecting, suspicious, mistrustful, apprehensive
What are their inner feelings? Angry, resentful, insecure, disappointed

Negative behavior: judging, criticizing, disapproving —
How do you perceive your spouse's behavior? Resentful, bitter, indignant
What are their inner feelings? Overly self-critical, insecure, angry

If you're good at reading between the lines, you'll notice that outer expressions of anger and sadness often emerge from inner feelings of insecurity or discontent. Think about the stresses in your life that cause you to be cranky, upset or just miserable to be around. Feelings of rejection are often scrambled in our inner world and then dished out at others who just happen to get in our way. All of us have bad days when we get upset at the people closest in our lives, but we are really just hurt by other circumstances such as getting yelled at by an angry boss, receiving a parking ticket or missing the bus. For a marriage to succeed, you need to know when your wife or husband is just having a bad day or if other "inner world issues" are not being met.

Let's take a look at some of the issues that can guide you through your spouse's inner world. They include:

- Self Esteem
- Individuality
- Love and Friendship
- Control
- Spirituality

At the end of each section is a relationship test question that can help you evaluate if you are sensitive to your spouse's emotional needs.

Self Esteem

Self esteem is one of the most important factors influencing human behavior. Despite what some people believe, self esteem can be a critical issue in marriage, where unresolved identity issues from childhood can place unwanted stress on a relationship.

Low self esteem can be very painful and difficult to overcome. Our sense of self esteem is something we come into the world with, which follows us through life like a shadow. If we lose it, we are lost. If we have it, we can face all of life's all of life's trials and tribulations and maintain our sense of satisfaction and emotional well-being. Most parents understand the role self esteem plays in childhood. When children grow up, we teach them how to take losses in stride and to learn how to win and lose with grace. We teach children that it's them, and not just their grades, that matter.

Once childhood passes, unresolved self esteem issues can last for a lifetime. For example, in marriages where one person suffers from low self esteem, they may feel that their spouse never properly fulfills their emotional needs. And, where both suffer from feelings of low self esteem, a husband and wife may feel perpetually disappointed in their relationship.

Expectations make this issue even more complex. Married couples tend to enter marriage with the belief that any hurt they may have experienced in the past will now be healed by their spouse. They may also hope that their spouse will somehow make them feel good about themselves and nurture their self image.

A couple once came to talk with me about difficulties they were having in their marriage. The issue that was burning in their minds was the negative behavior of their teenage son. The father found it difficult to parent his rebellious teenager with confidence, and the wife had given up hope in her children and in her marriage as well. Overall, they were both visibly angry at one another, withdrawn and disappointed in their relationship.

I sensed that there were more issues hiding under the surface. After exploring their histories, I discovered a complex history that pointed toward the issue of self esteem. The husband it turned out, had lost his mother at a young age and was raised by his father who was too preoccupied with their financial survival to pay much attention to his son's emotional needs. The wife had also had a very difficult childhood. She grew up with a father who had a temper and would often yell at her without reason. Early on, she had learned how to adapt and "disappear" from the house when he was around.

Years later, these two individuals would continue their childhood patterns and be caught in an endless cycle of emotional turmoil. Here is how the issue of self esteem spiraled out of control: whenever he sensed that his wife was not responsive to his emotional needs, he would start yelling at her. His wife, who was mistreated by her father and had learned how to avoid conflict, would physically and emotionally withdraw from him and try to hide from her husband's rage. This would then intensify his feelings of rejection and make him even angrier.

To break the cycle, I suggested that both husband and wife needed work in the area of self esteem. They could begin by exploring how their childhood traumas were now influencing their present-day behavior. Through becoming aware of these inner issues, they would be better equipped to respond to their deeper emotional wounds and start healing their feelings of rejection and neglect.

Here is a list of childhood family issues that may be interrupting your ability to have a happy marriage as an adult:

- Divorce
- Learning disabilities
- Lack of friendships
- Illness
- Physical or emotional abuse
- A sick parent
- A death in the family

There is no doubt that anyone who has experienced a divorce in their family may have feelings of low self esteem. Marital conflict affects people in various ways. Children who are exposed to conflict at home (which tends to coincide with a negative and hostile relationship between the parents) are more at risk for aggression, internalizing by withdrawing, depressive symptoms, and feelings of low self esteem.

Also, an adult who as a child has lost a parent may feel a sense of loss that can carry on for a lifetime. Losing someone at a young age can diminish self-confidence, create feelings of despair, and leave individuals with feelings of anxiety and uncertainty.

Part of the healing process is to become aware of these inner issues and to begin discussing them with one's spouse.

Talking about them in an honest and open way can help them become aware of each other's feelings of abandonment. Here are some tips on how to nourish each other's level of self esteem:

First Aid Relationship Tips

 Highlight positive aspects of their physical, mental, and emotional development, such as the way they look, the way they express their thoughts and feelings, the skills they have, and those they are developing.

 Focus on their accomplishments.

 Congratulate them for their achievements, however big or small. Remind them daily of the things they do well and of the courage they have shown.

 Help them to be realistic and accept the fact that, while they aren't perfect at everything, they don't have to be.

 Teach them to laugh at past disappointments when they can. Use setbacks as opportunities for insight and growth.

 Help them develop a support system of people they trust who will listen when they need to talk.

As the level of self esteem improves, many couples find their ability to have a successful marriage greatly enhanced.

Relationship Test: Self Esteem

Do you take time to develop your spouse's self esteem?

1   2   3   4   5

Never—Rarely —Constantly

Individuality

One of the most powerful dimensions of a successful marriage is a couple's ability to keep focused on each other's good points and unique personality traits. Too often, people become fixated on the negative. They "sweat over the small stuff," and forget about the positive points that brought them together in the first place.

When I'm told by couples who have been married for ten or twenty years that they have lost their loving feelings toward one another, I respond by saying that it's a matter of perspective. If they can change the way they view one another, they will also be able to change their feelings and actions. For example, when couples get married, most have an abundance of positive feelings toward each other. They are attracted to one another on an emotional and physical level. Yet, after time, feelings begin to change. Emotional inertia sets in that leaves them with a gnawing sense of rejection and disappointment. To get over the emotional hurdle, they need to shift gears and contemplate all the right reasons they got married in the first place. Ultimately, they need to focus on each other's unique qualities and highlight their individuality.

In counseling, I also help couples focus on their unique points by going back to the beginning of marriage and recalling with them the enthusiasm and exhilaration both had for one another. Reliving the engagement period is an easy way to get started. Most couples will fondly recall the excitement of shopping for their engagement ring. When they entered into the jewelry store, their eyes were drawn to the brilliance of precious stones, their unique sparkle, and the beauty of their settings which captured and displayed their radiance. Eventually they chose a ring that called out to them and said, "This one is unique, there is none other in the world like me."

The ring, I explain, is an appropriate metaphor for marriage. One starts a marriage feeling that they have chosen their special "ring," one so unique that it will never be found again. For the first few years, the ring maintains its sparkle. However, after five, ten or fifteen years, the brilliance can become dull. It's a fact of life that the human eye becomes weary of even the most beautiful objects. When we see something all the time, we tend to lose sight of its beauty; we tend to take it for granted. And when we do, the secret to a long and successful marriage is for each individual to remind themselves of the gem they found in the first place.

Shmuel, 30 and Rivka, 28, came to speak with me about their troubled marriage. He was a law student and rabbi, and she was an occupational therapist. Each was at the top of their class. They were charming, talented, and full of life, but somehow over the years, they lost their "spark," and were more focused on pointing out each other's faults instead of finding their strengths. A common interchange would revolve around her feelings that her husband had lost interest in their relationship and his feelings that she was overly critical of his behavior. They often fought about house cleaning, childrearing, and how money was being spent.

I suggested to Shmuel and Rivka that they needed to reexamine the reasons they got married in the first place. To start the process, I suggested that even the simplest objects can be enjoyed. Take a rose for example and stare at it for several minutes. Look at how its petals are perfectly placed next to one another. See how each petal reflects varying shades of red and blends precisely to the petal that gently rests beside it.

You see, the more you look closely at something as simple as a rose, the more beautiful it becomes. So too, in a relationship, a husband and wife need to think about their spouse's unique identity, and by doing so, begin to appreciate the special "one" that they married. They need to appreciate their spouse for who they are instead of what they expect them to be or not to be.

First Aid Relationship Tips

Think about all the positive qualities inherent in most individuals:

- Loving-kindness

- Sensitivity

- Flexibility

- Sense of humor

- Capacity to grow

- Parenting skills

- It's all about focusing on the good in one another and using that reference point to develop a better relationship.

Unfortunately, I have seen many couples who spend a significant amount of time nit picking about each other's faults. Instead, they need to change their lens of perception and view their spouse in a positive light.

Relationship Quiz

To change your perception of each other, I suggest making a list of your spouse's positive points. Here are some questions that can get you started:

What unique qualities does your spouse have?

What are his/her talents?

What can he/she do that you are unable to do yourself?

What tasks does he/she fulfill in the marriage that makes your life easier?

In what ways does he/she help you develop your own identity?

What acts of loving-kindness does he/she do for you, unnoticed?

With your new list you can review your spouse's good points every day. I even suggest keeping the list in your wallet, and glance at it every night before coming home from work. The "individuality" list can gives couples the energy needed to grow closer together each day.

Relationship Test: Individuality

How often do you nurture your spouse's awareness of his or her individuality?

1   2   3   4   5

Never   Rarely   Constantly

Love and Friendship

At the core of a good relationship is the quality of love and friendship shared between a husband and wife. Love is the glue that bonds couples together and keeps their marriage vibrant and alive.

Although our society overuses the world "love," it's probably one of the most talked about yet misunderstood concepts in marriage, and for sure it is one of the hardest emotions to maintain.

Every couple begins their marriage thinking that they are "in love." Of course, at the beginning, it's easy to share feelings of love when the relationship is fresh and exciting. But after several months or years — without paying attention to nurturing each other — feelings of love can fall to the wayside.

The best way to understand the nature of love is to ask couples who are happily married about the "secret" to love in their marriage. They will probably say that they don't take their spouse's love for granted; rather, they take time to build their relationship and deepen their commitment toward one another every day. They realize that love is something you have to give, not just something you feel. Love needs be expressed in tangible ways.

Take a few moments on the quality of love and affection in your relationship. Do you call each other from work to see how each spouse's day is going? Do you buy each other small gifts that let your spouse know you care? Do you make sure to buy them their favorite foods or bring home their favorite dessert from the store? Do you go out of your way to help clean up around the house, carry out the garbage, or do the dishes? These are all tangible acts of love that tell your spouse that you love and care about them.

And, let's not forget friendship, the other side of the marriage equation. Deep down inside, you are also your spouse's closest friend. You're the person they can rely on after a stressful day at work. You're also the most trusted person in their life when they need to share their hidden feelings, hurts, wishes and dreams. Think about all the positive and enjoyable experiences you have with your friends. You can rely on them when you're down and share a good laugh by just hanging out with each other and schmoozing. First and foremost, couples need to be friends and spend as much quality time together as possible. It's crucial to set aside time for each other to take a walk, go out for dinner or just talk. On your "dates" you need to do a lot of active listening, show empathy toward each other's pain, and try to laugh away some of life's greatest stresses.

In the long run, more relationship time spent together builds the foundation for more intimate expressions of love in marriage.

Relationship Test: Love and Friendship

How often do you nurture your spouse's need for love and friendship?

1   2   3   4   5

Never Rarely Constantly

Control

Every couple has questions about how to pay their bills, how to spend money, where to send their kids to school and what they do during their vacations. Some couples find negotiating their needs to be an easy task, while others constantly complain and say things like, "Why am I the one who always has to do this?" or, "Whose responsibility is this?" Every couple, however, must determine how to share power; some just do it more consciously than others.

Making decisions is often based upon who has control in the relationship. In some marriages, both husband and wife have found the balance between control and respect for one another. In other marriages, control is much more lopsided, where one spouse has the upper hand in one or more areas.

The problems begin when power is assumed by one side or the other, or when both sides have the same desire to control each other. When one spouse yields an inordinate amount of control over areas such as finances, education, food and vacation plans, and their spouse feels totally left out in the dark, the controlling spouse needs to moderate their desire in order to achieve a healthy balance of power in their relationship. He or she will need to learn how to compromise and negotiate what they want, and moderate their need to control.

Having a frank discussion about how decisions are made and who makes them is a good place to start. To do this, you need to start learning about the areas of control that your spouse feels are important in their life, and see if there is room for compromise.

Here are some possible areas where control matters most to your spouse:

- Money
- Education
- Parenting
- Vacation Plans
- In-Law Relationships

After identifying their needs, think about how important these issues are in your life. If for example, you both have a need to control money or your vacation plans, this may lead toward more conflict in those areas. One possible solution is to allow your spouse more control in those areas. Another approach is to have a frank discussion about the emotional issues underlying their need to control. Sometimes control is coming from a person's vision for how things "should" be, and he or she is moralizing about it and making you feel ashamed for not living up to their expectations. Other times, a desire to control emerges from a deeply-rooted sense of fear or abandonment, that somehow, if he or she is not in control of that area, their lives will fall apart. By controlling, they don't have to experience the discomfort of growing, changing, or stretching themselves. Instead, they can pretend that their world is logical, orderly, predictable, and safe.

Trying to identify your areas of control and your ability to compromise can reduce emotional conflicts in marriage. There is a fine balance, but once we find it, we are much happier, healthier and more capable of mature love in marriage.

Relationship Test: Control

How often do you ask your spouse about their control-needs in marriage?

1   2   3   4   5

Never   Rarely   Constantly

Spirituality

The fifth and perhaps deepest level of a person's inner world is their spiritual vision for life and for marriage. Spiritual principles help guide us and give us the strength and clarity to endure any difficulties that life may bring.

As most couples discover, even in the best situations, marriage is about dealing with changes, stress, the difficulties of parenting and trying to make a living. At the soul level, a person senses that there exists a higher purpose in life, and that their life is driven by principles that are not limited by their daily pressures and never-ending responsibilities.

A person's sense of spirituality goes beyond their thoughts and feelings and touches upon their soul. According to the Torah, the soul's deepest desire is to connect to G-d and fulfill His commandments, independent of any impediments it may face along the way. It also desires to unite with its other half — its soul mate — and accomplish its mission together. Only through marriage can we fulfill special commandments such as having children, building a Jewish home, and creating an environment that enhances our spiritual existence.

Shared spiritual values also make marriage more enjoyable. Celebrating Shabbos together, and sharing life-cycle events such as Bar Mitzvahs, Weddings and Bris Milahs, brings couples together and highlights their common goals and aspirations. It also connects them with their community through synagogue attendance and by participating in other organizational activities where they share their values with other like-minded individuals.

The spirituality achieved in marriage also goes far beyond the couple. Their spiritual bonds give their children a sense of meaning in their lives. They grow up knowing that their lives are a part of an historical continuum which began on Mount Sinai, and which will guide them throughout their lives.

I often suggest to couples to explore their shared spiritual vision of the marriage and examine the spiritual reasons that brought them together in the first place. Many couples, for instance, spend a year or more studying in yeshiva and seminary in Israel. Some dedicate several years learning in kollel and building a spiritual foundation for their marriage. Others dedicate their lives early on in their marriage and become rabbis, teachers or organization leaders in their community.

A couple's commitment toward Jewish learning and community values establishes their deeply held spiritual values, as they choose a life of leadership and service of others. Often it's these formative years of learning that define a couple's future spiritual values, which last for a lifetime. Some couples, however, have trouble maintaining their spiritual vision, and become too focused on their daily pressures. These couples need to regain their spiritual leanings by exploring their spiritual values together. The following questions can help couples improve their understanding of one another:

What are the spiritual principles that formed the basis of your marriage?

Have your principles changed or advanced? What are your spiritual desires in life now?

In what ways do you feel that your spiritual desires have remained unexpressed?

How can you be of help to your spouse to enhance his/her spiritual ambitions in life?

When couples explore their spiritual values together, they can enhance their feelings of love toward one another and increase their commitment to their marriage.

Relationship Test: Spirituality

How often do you discuss the spiritual foundations of your marriage?

1   2   3   4   5

Never Rarely Constantly

Relationship Test Results

Now go back and add up your numbers for all five of the relationship tests. The test is a measuring stick that can help you evaluate how responsive you are to your spouse's needs. If you scored below 10, then clearly the bonds of your relationship may be weak and you need to spend time nurturing your connection. If you scored above 10, then you have a greater chance of breaking through into your spouse's emotional world. If you scored 20 or above, then you are doing a great job and you should continue to strengthen the quality of your relationship.

By increasing a connection to your spouse's inner world you can forge a greater sense of closeness, develop mutual respect, and learn how to speak their "emotion-language," which is the key to solving problems and growing closer together.

Putting It All Together

Let's take a look at how understanding these five levels can help improve marriage. The following are examples of how couples improved their relationships, by uncovering the secrets of their spouses' inner worlds.

Self Esteem

Yaakov, 37 and Avivah, 32, were married for twelve years and had four children ages 14, 12, 9 and 7. Yaakov was a graphic artist who worked long and hard hours at his company, and Avivah was a high school teacher in the local Hebrew academy.

Over the years an unresolved problem was lingering in their marriage. Their 12 and 9 year old boys were both diagnosed with learning disabilities and needed costly remedial help.

Yaakov and Avivah were overwhelmed by the pressure of paying for their children's education and dealing with the daily stress of their sons' learning disabilities. But that was not all. What started as a financial problem had deeper emotional underpinnings. Their children's learning disabilities turned out to be just one part of the problem. During numerous therapy sessions with the family, it was revealed that Yaakov, too, had various undetected learning issues and adult ADHD. When he was a child, he found it hard to concentrate in school, and now as an adult he continued to suffer silently at work and in any intellectual environment that required his attention.

For years Yaakov tried hiding his problems, rationalizing that he just felt "nervous" before tests and jittery whenever he would be asked to speak in public. Yaakov had a real emotional disability that caused him to become shy in front of other men and in any situation where he would be asked to perform an intellectual task like answering questions on a test or learning Talmud with a chevrusah.

Due to his secret problem, Yaakov avoided helping his children with their homework. He would usually tell them that he was too busy with his own work and pass the responsibility onto his wife.

Avivah couldn't handle the pressure and was resentful that Yaakov was abdicating responsibility for their children's education. She also believed that her husband was a failure and could never live up to her expectations.

I believed that Yaakov's little secret had turned into an emotionally disruptive pattern in his life. His learning disability had affected his sense of self esteem. And it was no wonder. Imagine spending 12 years in school and being unable to decipher what one's teachers were writing on the board, or the pain of consistently failing test after test and only achieving a C- as your highest mark. There was no question that his learning problems had turned into self esteem issues later on in life.

I tried focusing Avivah's attention on the need to find ways to work on boosting Yaakov's feelings of self esteem, and suggested that she take the following steps:

1. Reduce criticism of Yaakov when he can't help the children do their homework.

2. Hire a tutor who can assist their children at night.

3. Using Active Listening skills, talk to Yaakov about his learning disability without denying his feelings.

4. Highlight Yaakov's other great skills and talents as an artist, a loving husband and caring parent.

Avivah needed to focus on the positive contributions Yaakov was making as a parent, such as his kind and loving attitude toward his children, his ability to work hard and support their family, and his warm and loving attitude toward her as his wife. Focusing on the negative would only make Yaakov feel worse and push him to withdraw even further away from her.

After a few sessions in counseling, Yaakov and Avivah began implementing the first "C" of Relationship Theory: Connection. Eventually, Avivah began to connect to Yaakov's inner world and to develop his level of self esteem, which could allow Yaakov to feel less ashamed of his disability. With an improved self image, Yaakov could feel at ease with himself and more confident as a parent, which would bring all of them more happiness in their lives.

Individuality

Chaim, 45, and Rivkah, 42, came to speak with me about "personality" differences in their marriage. There was no doubt that their personalities were just about at opposite ends of the spectrum. Chaim was a tall and sharply-dressed individual whose presence demanded respect when he walked into the room. Rivkah was almost the opposite, dressed in colorful layers of pastel clothes, a draped tichel, and Birkenstocks. They were the classic Type "A" meets Type "B," couple who broke all stereotypes when it came to compatibility.

It wasn't a surprise to me when Rivkah began the session by explaining that they were having serious trouble communicating with one another. According to Rivkah, they were experiencing constant emotional friction in the marriage. Chaim was a well-respected rebbe in the community, and was engrossed day and night in either teaching his students or learning with his chevrusah. Due to his demanding schedule there was very little communication in the marriage, especially at night when he would arrive home at around ten o'clock, eat dinner and fall right to asleep. Although Rivkah would attempt to speak with him, Chaim tended to act distant, cold and unemotional. She felt lonely and needed a close emotional relationship; one that Chaim seemed unwilling or unable to give her.

Their problems didn't stop there. Chaim saw the situation from a totally different perspective. He felt that his wife was unwilling to help him fulfill his commitment to Torah learning, and that she had forgotten the reason they got married. Originally, Rivkah was supportive of Chaim's rigorous schedule. Now she seemed to be hostile to the idea that he could leave the house every night for his chevrusah.

Chaim was also bothered by his wife's personality and believed that she was too "spiritual." He also felt that Rivkah was spending too much time reading psychology books and self-help articles, and that these were having a negative influence on her religious beliefs.

I suggested to Chaim and Avivah that they needed to assess how they viewed their diverse emotional tendencies. One thing was for sure: both Chaim and Avivah had a strong tendency toward individualism. For example, Chaim believed that his raison d'être was learning Torah. Avivah, however, believed that her life's calling was to heal the world, and to discover her destiny through exploring spiritual themes in Judaism and psychology. Outwardly, these would seem to be two divergent pathways that would lead toward opposite destinations. On the one hand, a life of learning takes discipline and requires a considerable amount of time and effort. On the other hand, a "spiritual" or sensitive person tends to thrive on conversation, acts of compassion, and connecting to people around them.

Instead of a clash of wills, I suggested that Chaim and Avivah look at their unique traits as special ingredients needed to create a vibrant relationship. Both characteristics could be viewed as necessary to raise a healthy family and sustain a successful marriage. Chaim needed to view Avivah's spiritual-yet-different approach to life as complimenting his own. Her warm and nurturing personality nurtured their children, and could compensate for his rigorous learning schedule outside of their home. Avivah was the kind of person that everyone felt comfortable talking to about their hopes, fears and deepest emotions. Her abilities to listen and empathize were important skills needed to raise their children.

Chaim, on the other hand, had different strengths. He had the fortitude to maintain a demanding learning schedule and believed that Torah study needed to be the most important occupation in life. He was willing to lose sleep in order to maintain his early-morning shiurim and late-night lectures.

Avivah had married a unique individual whose life's mission was to keep the passion of Torah study burning and to be a living role model to his children and students. Her life — and the lives of their children and his numerous students — would be enriched by Chaim's devout and impressive commitment to Torah study. He had a special drive that would keep him focused on his core values, independent of the multiple financial and personal challenges facing his idealist lifestyle.

Avivah's challenge was not an easy one. Chaim's demanding schedule would require her to lead a more independent lifestyle than most women in her community. And her sacrifices would involve additional challenges. At times she would have feelings of loneliness and frustration. Both she and Chaim would need to overcome their daily stresses by making their "together" time more enjoyable and meaningful. To accomplish this, I suggested to Chaim that he needs to practice active listening and to start hearing his wife's inner messages. Chaim would also need to tell his wife more frequently how much he appreciated her patience and her commitment to his learning. She needed to feel that although he wasn't at home as much as she wanted, he was always thinking about her.

In their case, they both had unique talents that could be combined to enhance a special relationship. The challenge would be to view each other's differences as strengths and their individual points as opportunities for growth. By focusing on their individuality, their marriage could then head in the right direction.

Control

Simon, 36 and Ronit, 33 had just celebrated their third wedding anniversary, and came to speak with me about tension in their marriage. Simon was a successful businessman, and Ronit was a hard-working paralegal in a high-powered law firm. They were a "super couple" who believed they were able to achieve just about any goal they wanted in life. Simon and Ronit were thriving in just about every area of their lives except for one: Simon and Ronit each had highly controlling personalities, which would tarnish and strain a potentially great marriage. Their relationship was filled with high expectations and intense feelings of disappointment leading to intense marital conflict.

Adding to their stress was the dysfunctional relationship Ronit had with her parents. Ronit's parents were troubled individuals. Her father was a doctor and her mother was his secretary. Their lives had revolved around his medical practice and his duties as chief of surgery at a local hospital. Busy with their work, her parents paid little attention to her emotional needs. For example, her father frequently would go on lengthy business trips to surgical hospitals around the world that would last two to three months at a time. During those lonely periods, Ronit's mother would suffer from bouts of depression, and would neglect caring for Ronit and her siblings. Her father was also very controlling with money and refused to give his children tuition for college, even forcing them to take on menial jobs to pay for school. His behavior bordered on being abusive, and his children would spend many years suffering inside from the emotional damage caused by his controlling and manipulative behavior.

Ronit's emotional baggage was only one part of the problem. About one month after giving birth, Ronit's brother, Avram, came to visit them. It was by all accounts a tension-filled visit. Ronit and her brother had never had a good relationship, but what would occur that trip would change their family forever. Her brother was a high-strung college-age student who was emotionally tense and known for his immature outbursts.

Simon was holding their newborn son when Avram started criticizing him about their lifestyle, claiming that Simon wasn't taking proper care of his sister. His comments made Ronit very upset. She was trying hard to mend the relationship with her parents and Avram was inflaming an already fragile situation. Ronit then pulled Simon into the kitchen and asked him to speak to Avram. Afterwards, Simon approached Avram and asked that he behave in a more respectful manner in their home, and mentioned that Ronit's family had given him the wrong impression of their lifestyle. He also said that Avram's parents were inappropriately criticizing them and creating animosity between Ronit and her siblings. At that point, in a blind rage of anger, Ronit's brother punched Simon in the face and stomach, throwing him backwards onto the stone floor, still holding the baby in his arms. Luckily, the baby was unhurt. But the emotional and physical pain would continue to affect Simon long after the event.

Ronit and Simon were overwhelmed by the emotions surrounding the attack, and the overall stress from dealing with angry and dysfunctional in-laws. Ronit was torn between her relationship with her parents and her marriage with Simon.

Now, they wanted to know from me how to respond to her family, and how to deal with their emotions.

In my estimation Simon and Ronit were both dealing with questions of control in their marriage, which was manifested in the following ways:

1. Ronit held a deeply-seated desire to control her family's behavior.

2. Simon believed that he could control Ronit's family to be more accepting of him and Ronit.

3. Ronit and Simon both tried to control each other's levels of affection toward one another. If Simon, for instance, didn't respond automatically to her bids for affection she would take it personally and act critically toward him.

Although this was a very painful and difficult situation, I believed that Ronit and Simon needed to see how they were caught up in the circle of control. The circle had begun many years earlier with Ronit's father trying to control his own family. Ronit would then continue this pattern, by trying to control her father's behavior in turn. Finally, Simon was drawn into the circle and was trying to control both Ronit and her parents.

To recover from the trauma of the attack, Ronit and Simon would have to reduce their tendencies to control, and focus on putting their relationship at the center of their lives. To begin with, Ronit's parents were now of secondary importance in her life. Her marriage to Simon was really what counted, not resolving her childhood conflict with her mother and father and pitting Simon against her family. Ronit needed to give up the wish that her parents would somehow start loving her and Simon. She could, however, choose to make Simon a greater emotional priority in her life, and focus on his needs rather than on her parents' demands.

After several sessions, Simon and Ronit began to moderate their desires to control their families and each other. They also began to shift from control to mutual respect, and focused on their relationship, which is the key to living beyond the moment.

First Aid Relationship Tips

 Search beyond external behaviors and seek inner motivations.

 Learn about your spouse's inner world.

 Talk to your spouse about their emotional needs.

First Aid Exercise 2: Emphasizing Affirmation and Mutual Self-Esteem Building

Something I love about you that I haven't told you before is…

One thing I'd like to happen for you this year is…

A time I felt very "close" to you was…

I remember many times I have been proud of you. One was…

One of the things I value most in our marriage is…

A commitment I'd like to make to you to help our relationship grow is…

Something that makes me feel good about us and our marriage is…

I feel good when I look toward the future because I see us…

I think of fun times I have had with you. One was…

If we could start a vacation tomorrow – just the two of us – I would like…

First Aid Exercise 3: Mutual Support – Affirmation Exercise
List your three most important personal goals in life: 1. 2. 3. Predict what you think are your spouse's top personal goals in life: 1. 2. 3. List three specific things (big or small) you would like your spouse to do to help you. 1. 2. 3. Predict three specific things you believe your spouse would like you to do to help him/her. 1. 2. 3.

CHAPTER 3
THE ART OF
COMMUNICATION

In This Chapter:

- The power of active listening
- The ten commandments of communication
- Learning to say that you're sorry
- Communicating feelings in common situations
- Examining your communication system

David and his wife had been married for 15 years and believed they knew what each other really wanted. While attending a marriage seminar on communication, David and his wife listened to the instructor declare, "It is essential that husbands and wives know the things that are important to each other."

He addressed the man, "Can you describe your wife's favorite flower?"

David leaned over, touched his wife's arm gently and whispered, "Pillsbury All-Purpose, isn't it?"

Sometimes we think that someone is saying one thing, when actually, their message is completely different. Good communication, in all spheres of life, necessitates that you pick up on each other's subtle signs and understand the feelings and emotions behind their words.

A few years ago when I was looking to buy a new car, I spotted a sign at a local car dealer that read "Brand New Sedans at Low, Low Prices." Enthusiastically, I walked in expecting to find the ride of my life. Within seconds, a blue sedan caught my eye, and I quickly hopped into the driver's seat, started playing with the console, and sunk into the extra-plush leather seats. I knew right away that I found the car I was looking for. At least that's what I thought.

Suddenly, a car salesman woke me out of my almost dream-like state.

"These cars are not for sale. I think you made a mistake," the assertive salesman said to me.

"Mistake?" I replied, "I couldn't be happier."

"Are you sure you don't want something else? How about a larger minivan with a CD player — something your kids would love," he asked.

"No thanks. We already have a Town and Country. I'm looking for something for myself."

"Yourself? I guess you think one van is enough for the family."

"Of course ONE is enough. Can't you just show me a similar sedan to the one I want?"

"Well, we have smaller sedans, but they are pre-owned."

"Pre-owned. You mean secondhand, right?"

"That's what we call it in our industry, 'pre-owned.'"

"But I want a new car!"

"Okay, I get it. You want a new sedan."

"That's right. Do you have any?"

"Well, we used to. Now we have compacts and minivans. Are you sure we can't find a real deal for you?"

Like most unsuspecting car buyers, I walked out disappointed and downright annoyed that I was saying one thing and he was hearing another. In fact, we were speaking two totally different languages. He assumed that he knew what I wanted, but in truth, he was only interested in fulfilling his own narrow agenda.

Couples often fall into this same pattern of speaking without first listening to what their spouse is trying to tell them.

They make the mistake of assuming one thing when their spouse's mind is moving in the opposite direction.

First Aid Relationship Tips

So what are the ways couples can improve their ability to communicate effectively in marriage and create a language of love? According to the latest theories in communication, the most important areas of focus are:

- Learning how to actively listen

- Mirroring your spouse's feelings

- Empathizing

- Hearing feelings behind words

- Reducing criticism

- Learning to say that you're sorry

Active Listening

One of the most essentials techniques in improving communication is active listening. Active listening, as opposed to simple listening, is a style of communication where couples pay close attention to each other's words and feelings. Instead of assuming that they automatically catch their message, they go the extra mile to listen carefully to their spouse's "inner" voice. Active listening encourages people to download their thoughts to someone who will listen without being judgmental.

Imagine how good it feels when you are listened to, by someone who matters in your life. Everyone feels comforted when a good friend, teacher or spouse spends a few minutes listening to what you have to say. That's because good communicators perceive communication as a two-way street, where listening is as equally important as is speaking one's mind. Unfortunately, many people believe that the purpose of communication is to simply get another person to do what you want. From their perspective, communication is merely a way to achieve certain goals, such as acquiring possessions, making money, attaining valuable services, and so on. Yet, in marriage, communicating is about more than just achieving an end; it's a means to achieving a closer and more intimate relationship.

There are three major components to active listening:

- Mirror your spouse's feelings
- Empathize with your spouse
- Detect the feelings behind their words.

Mirror Your Spouse's Feelings

Mirroring is a good way to start actively listening to each other. To mirror, you simply paraphrase or repeat back to your spouse what they are saying to you. For example, if one day he/she comes home and says to you: "I had a horrible day at work!" you reflect on their words by saying, "It sounds like you had a terrible day at work." Don't try to editorialize or deny what they are saying. Instead, allow them to fully express their feelings, and encourage more communication by paraphrasing what they just said to you. Or, if they had a hard day at school and their students drove them crazy, you can let them know that you hear what they are going through by saying, "It sounds like your kids drove you crazy today." Most of the time, validating their feelings is really what they need from you.

Think about the last time you were frustrated and you tried to share your feelings with your parents or friends. What kind of response was more soothing? If they dismissed your feelings and said, "Oh, don't worry about it. Tomorrow will be better,"? Or, if they gently mirrored your words back to you and said, "It sounds like you had a hard day," or, "That sounds rough. Can you tell us more about your feelings?" Most people appreciate when their feelings are validated and that someone is willing to listen to their pain or frustration.

The difference between the two styles is quite distinct, as the following two dialogues reveal.

Relationship Skills

In the first conversation, Rivkah doesn't utilize the principles of active listening.

Chaim: I'm furious! I had a lousy day at work!

Rivkah: What? Were you late for work again?

Chaim: What are you talking about?

Rivkah: I told you last night to go to bed earlier and leave on time.

Chaim: That has nothing to do with it. It's my boss. He's out of his mind again. He is nervous about our deadline and feels that our department isn't keeping up.

Rivkah: Well, I keep on telling you that you guys have to keep ahead or else.

Chaim: Give me a break! We are working as hard as possible!

Rivkah: I guess it's not enough.

Chaim: How much can I possibly do?!

In the following conversation, Rivkah has learned the skills needed to be a good active listener, and she mirrors her husband's feelings.

Chaim: I'm furious! I had a lousy day at work!

Rivkah: You had a lousy day.

Chaim: My boss was impossible! He has such a temper!

Rivkah: He was angry today?

Chaim: He couldn't stop ranting and raving about performance.

Rivkah: Hmm. He's worried about your performance.

Chaim: Give me a break! We are working as hard as possible!!

Rivkah: You feel you are working as hard as possible. I'm sure you are trying your best.

Chaim: Of course we are. We are getting glitches all along the way from distributors.

Rivkah: You are frustrated with your distributors.

Chaim: Of course. I can't control what they do. But my boss doesn't care about reality.

Rivkah: You can't control them or your boss either.

Chaim: That's right. I feel so out of control.

Rivkah: That must be frightening and downright frustrating.

Chaim: I'm feeling out of control and I'm really scared about the future.

Through active listening, Rivkah was able to avoid pouring gasoline on an already explosive issue. Her husband was feeling overwhelmed with work stress, and it wasn't only with his boss, but with the distributors as well. Instead of criticizing or dismissing her husband's behavior and feelings, she aimed to listen to his inner message and uncover his more vulnerable emotions of fear and frustration. Practicing this kind of communication helps build a caring relationship — one that will enable more positive interactions and dialogue in other key areas of life.

Empathize With Your Spouse

To feel loved and nurtured your spouse needs to feel that you empathize with their emotions. The key is empathy. Empathy isn't the same as sympathy or pity. It means being able to put yourself in another's position, to feel what they feel and see what they see, without losing yourself in the process. And it means you do all of that, even though you may disagree with your spouse's perceptions, opinions, or feelings. Take a few minutes a day, at a time that works best for both of you, to empathize with the stresses and strains you are each experiencing in other areas of your life. It can make a difference between a marriage that succeeds, and one that fails.

Through empathy you can deepen the effect of active listening and make your spouse feel that they can turn to you whenever they need to. Empathizing means that we listen without judging the other person's thoughts and feelings. We tell them that we understand what they are facing and share their pain.

Here are two scenarios that contrast empathetic versus non-empathetic communication.

Relationship Skills

In the first conversation, Shlomo goes on the attack with Batya, and forgets that she is just looking for someone to empathize with her feelings, not solve them.

Batya: I'm so upset at my sister for not inviting our entire family to the simcha. I can't believe she would hurt us like this.

Shlomo: She's terrible! I can't stand when she plays her games.

Batya: You better believe it. Last year we spent so much money on her visit, to make her happy, and now she does this? I'm really angry.

Shlomo: We spend so much on her. Why can't she reciprocate!?

Batya: She always plays games like this. I never know where she is coming from.

Shlomo: Yeah. She has done this so many times before. I'm getting used to it.

Batya: That's right. She has always behaved like this. I remember when we were little kids she would make sure to hog the nosh before anyone else did. She would just grab the pack of treats and eat them in her room, so nobody could see.

Shlomo: I told you. She is a grabber and cant control herself!

Batya: Right, just like now. She doesn't think of other people's feelings.

Shlomo: She never does.

Batya: I am so hurt!

In the following dialogue, Shlomo utilizes the power of empathy to relate to his wife's feelings.

Batya: I'm so upset at my sister for not inviting our entire family to the simcha. I can't believe she would hurt us like this.

Shlomo: You're feeling hurt by your sister.

Batya: You better believe it. Last year we spent so much money on her visit, to make her happy, and now she does this? I'm really angry!

Shlomo: We spend a lot of money, and now she tells you we can't come.

Batya: She always plays games like this. I never know where she is coming from!

Shlomo: You don't trust her and you don't understand how she makes decisions.

Batya: That's right. She has always behaved like this. I remember when we were little kids she would make sure to hog the nosh before anyone else did. She would just grab things and hide in her room, eating them.

Shlomo: She grabbed things before you had a fair chance.

Batya: Right, just like now. She doesn't think of other people's feelings.

Shlomo: You feel she doesn't care about you.

Batya: That's right. I wish she would be more sensitive to my feelings.

Shlomo: I understand.

Being empathetic takes time and effort. To deepen your level of empathy, here are some of the dos and don'ts that can make a difference:

Empathy Don'ts

- Don't ignore what your spouse is saying.

- Don't diminish the importance of your spouse's concerns:

- "What's the problem?" "Don't be so sensitive!"

- Don't rush to fix the problem: "Well, if I were you I'd..." or, "You should have..." Many people mistakenly believe that downplaying worries or offering advice is helpful. In fact, pat reassurances often magnify negative feelings, since they force a person to try even harder to feel acknowledged.

Empathy Do's

Do pay attention. Set aside the newspaper and turn off the TV when your spouse is talking.

- Do validate feelings. "He gave that special assignment to the new recruit? I can see why you're annoyed."

- Do ask questions with genuine interest. Make sure your spouse knows you heard what he or she has said. "So how did you respond to him?"

- Do respond with affection, understanding, and support:

- "I'm really sorry you have to put up with that." "Oh, sweetheart, that could happen to anyone. Don't be so hard on yourself."

- Do show support. Take your spouse's side. "I think your boss went a little overboard, too," is appropriate. "Well, you shouldn't have been late in the first place," isn't.

Hear Feelings Behind Words

Behind every word is a feeling that may be hiding below the surface. A wife or husband who listens carefully and detects these feelings goes right to the heart of the matter, and addresses their spouse's true inner needs. Good active listeners are able to help their spouse identify their feelings and give them ample opportunities to express their thoughts without being judged or criticized.

When a person comes home from work and is feeling angry or sad, there are probably a myriad of thoughts and emotions running through their mind. Here are several examples of feelings that lie below the surface. See if you can pick up on the possible inner feelings behind a person's behavior.

External Behavior	Inner Feelings
Angry	Irritated, hostile, annoyed
Depressed	Disappointed, ashamed, guilty
Upset	Indecisive, embarrassed, hesitant, shy
Helpless	Alone, fatigued, inferior, useless
Afraid	Fearful, nervous, panicky, restless, anxious
Hurt	Dejected, rejected, offended, deprived

Sad	Anguished, desperate, pessimistic, unhappy, lonely

So when a person is depressed, for example, getting down to their core emotions requires you to peel back layer after layer, to uncover their feelings of being disappointed, or perhaps being ashamed of their behavior. With each new layer you will inevitably uncover vulnerable and delicate feelings that touch upon the core of their psyche. This process may be painful — for both the one talking and the one listening — but to help one another you need to allow painful emotions to be released. It takes times and effort to get to the middle. You can't rush and "cut in," or you'll be left with broken pieces.

It's all about getting to the heart of the problem. For example, if a husband comes home from work one day and his wife says to him, "I'm overloaded! I can't take the kids anymore. Dinner isn't ready, the baby is running around without a diaper and the six-year-old won't do his homework!" It's natural to give a knee-jerk response like, "Okay. Just calm down; you're overreacting," or, "I will take charge. Go lay down. You need a break!" Either way, the husband is not practicing active listening. He defensively believes that his wife is communicating with him to get him to change the situation. But the truth is that she simply craves for him to hear the feelings hiding behind her words. She may appear to be angry, yet in actuality, she is feeling alone, fatigued and overwhelmed.

Putting It All Together

Here are more examples of couples facing situations where they need to learn how to apply the lessons of active listening. Read carefully as the active listener keeps the key principles in mind and builds a closer relationship with their spouse.

Chani: I can't believe that Leah failed another spelling test today.

Shaul: She did? What's wrong with her? She's not studying?

Chani: She wastes so much time on the phone with friends or surfing the web. And, you are also part of the problem, I asked you so many times to do homework with her, but you never do.

Shaul: Why do you think it's my fault?!

Chani: Well, you don't give her enough attention.

Shaul: Enough attention? How much can I give? You know how busy I am. I get home every night at 7:30. I need to eat dinner and unwind, and before you know it, Leah has to go to bed. I think it's the teacher's fault. You'd better call the teacher and figure this one out, before she fails the year.

Chani: I've called her twice and she hasn't returned my call. I think she's trying to ignore me.

Shaul: I never liked her. She only calls back her favorites. I guess she doesn't care about Leah.

Chani: The school doesn't care about us either. They only call you back if you're rich.

Shaul: Yeah, I guess we don't really matter!

In the following example, Shaul uses active listening to calm down the situation and get into a proactive mode.

Chani: Leah failed another spelling test today.

Shaul: She failed the test.

Chani: She wastes so much time on the phone with friends or surfing the web. And you're also part of the problem. I asked you so many times to do homework with her.

Shaul: You think it's my fault also.

Chani: Well, you don't give her any attention.

Shaul: You feel that Leah is failing because I don't give her enough time when I'm home.

Chani: Of course. She needs more attention from you. I can only give her so much at the end of the day. I'm losing my mind.

Shaul: I can see you are really overwhelmed.

Chani: I'm feeling terrible. Her teacher doesn't care about her. Neither does the school. What are we going do?

Shaul: Let's try to figure out what's really going on with Leah. Maybe she is feeling bad about herself. Perhaps she got hurt in school by one of her friends.

Chani: It's possible.

Shaul: How about a tutor? I know I found tutors very helpful in high school.

Chani: Okay. I'll talk to her.

Notice how Shaul really listens to what Chani is saying. He allows Chani to speak about Leah's problems without criticizing her. He empathizes with her feelings of rejection, but doesn't play into her damaging conclusions. Shaul tries to get to the heart of the matter by seeking out Chani's deep-seated feelings that exist behind her words. By practicing active listening, Shaul is building trust and communicating to Chani that she can always talk about what is upsetting her, and he will always be there to lend a listening ear.

Active listening is only one part of the marriage equation; learning what to say and what not to say is the other half. And, it's not just about expressing your feelings, but doing it in a way that avoids hurting the other person.

Some people are natural communicators. They know how to get across their point of view without damaging their relationship. Others (probably most of us) need some guidance on where to focus and what to steer clear of. If you are looking to learn communication skills that make a difference, the Ten Commandments of Communication offer timeless principles that can help.

The reason I call them "commandments," is to stress the idea that most people would never think of transgressing the basic principles of our faith like killing, stealing or breaking the Shabbos. Yet, how many couples find it difficult to avoid criticizing each other (and find it difficult to instead use endearing words on a consistent basis)? Couples need a short list of the dos and don't of how to communicate.

The Ten Commandments of Communication are based upon two principles: (1) to avoid the damaging effects of critical language; and (2) to focus on positive and nurturing words.

On one tablet are five Thou Shalt Nots:

1. Insult
2. Judge
3. Blame
4. Insinuate
5. Criticize

On the other tablet are five Thou Shalts:

5. Compliment
6. Be compassionate
7. Empathize
8. Validate
9. Nurture
10. Listen

In order to not transgress the rules of your relationship, avoid using the kinds of words listed in the Thou Shalt Nots. Couples who insult, judge or blame one another damage their relationship and cause unneeded stress to their marriage. In addition, those who insinuate, or who embarrass each other will deplete their emotional savings accounts and cause lasting damage to their relationship. No one likes being criticized, blamed, or belittled for their behavior, especially in marriage, where close daily contact necessitates a high level of sensitivity and understanding.

To make a marriage great, you need to fulfill the Thou Shalts. They focus on positive and nurturing statements that are caring and empathetic. The Thou Shalts encourage couples to empathize and find the good in one another. They are as important to human relationships as are the commandments to believe in G-d, and to not worship idols, important to Judaism and to our relationship with our Creator.

To evaluate how you're communicating in your marriage I suggest you periodically take a moment to see if you are following the Ten Commandments of Communication. Are your words accepting, friendly, compassionate, and understanding? Or, are they critical, aggressive, insulting or belittling? By looking at the ten commandments you can see whether you are transgressing the Thou Shalt Nots or fulfilling the Thou Shalts of communication. If the overall tone of your conversations is angry, critical, or confrontational, you are probably transgressing the Thou Shalt Nots. If you are using affirmative and encouraging words then you are fulfilling the positive emotional "mitzvos" for one another, and growing closer together each day.

Beginning your conversations with the right attitude is one way to fulfill the "commandments." In the same way that we meditate about the greatness of G-d and our love for Him before we pray, couples should also arouse a love for one another and think about the importance of their relationship before they speak. The inner message is, "I love you and care about you, and I want to deepen our relationship." When you begin with the right intention, you'll have a greater chance of using words that build happiness in your marriage. Having the right inner message may be your best guide in evaluating whether what you are about to say will push your spouse further away or bring him or her closer.

The following principles can also be helpful:

1. Soften your approach to the argument. Be less confrontational in your responses. Instead, make your tone with your spouse soft and tender so your spouse will feel secure. Avoid criticism at all costs! Spouses cannot connect when they tear each other down.

2. Validate what your spouse is feeling, instead of criticizing.

3. Listen sincerely to your spouse. Hear what he or she is really saying.

4. Show an understanding of the heart. Put yourself in your spouse's shoes while listening intently to what he or she says. Then communicate that you see the problem from his/her perspective. Put the argument on common ground by agreeing, "This is our problem."

5. Be willing to compromise. The relationship is far more important than the issue.

6. Give your spouse attention and affection. Try to communicate statements like, "I'm here and I'm not leaving." Point out the positive changes your spouse has made in your life.

7. Don't be afraid to laugh!

Learning to Say That You're Sorry

In marriage, it's inevitable that sometimes couples will step on each other's toes; especially during the first year of marriage, where newlyweds find themselves tip-toeing around their spouse's emotional roadblocks. Don't forget that it takes time to learn about your spouse's idiosyncrasies and to learn how to respond in a way that makes them feel at ease.

Here are some of the common mistakes people make in marriage:

- You forget about an important appointment and your spouse is furious

- You make up a time they will call you on your cell phone and you forget to turn on the phone.

- You invite your in-laws for dinner and forget to tell your spouse.

- You forget to bring her flowers for Shabbos or Yom Tov.

- You leave the dishes piled up in the sink.

Despite your mistakes, you can still undo your past actions by learning how to say, "'I'm' sorry."

Saying that you are sorry is so powerful that many couples have told me that it's the secret to having a long-lasting marriage, as the following story that appeared in a British newspaper points out.

"A British couple who hold the world record for the longest marriage said that their success was down to a glass of whisky, a glass of sherry and the word, "Sorry."

Percy and Florence Arrowsmith married on June 1, 1925 and will celebrate their 80th anniversary on Wednesday.

The Guinness World Records said that the couple held the title for the longest marriage and also for the oldest married couple's aggregate age.

"I think we're very blessed," said Florence, 100 years old. "We still love one another, that's the most important part."

Asked for their secret, Florence said you must never be afraid to say, "Sorry."

"You must never go to sleep bad friends," she said, while Percy, 105, said his secret to marital bliss was just two words: "yes dear."

The couple has three children, six grandchildren and nine great-grandchildren and are planning a party soon."

How to say that you're sorry

There are many ways to tell your significant other that you are sorry. To begin with, start by expressing your spouse that you genuinely feel sorry for your behavior, actions, or words.

"Please forgive my outburst, I do love and respect you and didn't mean to speak to you like that."

"I do love you and I can't stand fighting with you. Please forgive my part in all this. I want us to speak calmly and with respect for each other."

"I am very sorry, please forgive my tone of voice. I love you and don't want us to continue speaking to each other this way."

"I'm sorry. I love you and I am overreacting. Let's take a break right now so we can both calm down."

Second, it is very important to state that you are taking responsibility for your actions and not trying to justify your behavior or make excuses for it. If you don't take responsibility for your actions then your apology will have little value. You should also try to convey that your sincerely regret what you did. Many times, someone may simply say they are sorry to try to keep the peace and end an argument and they are not generally feeling remorse for their behavior. A genuine expression of sorrow for your behavior can mean a lot to the other person.

Michael, 32, and Rivkah, 29 learned about the need to say, "I'm sorry," the hard way. Michael was a well-respected accountant who worked in a high-pressure job. He usually worked late hours, and looked forward to unwinding at home — but not to be greeted by a loud choir of children when he entered the door.

A common scenario unfolded each night when Michael would return home from work and be greeted by his ready-for-bed children and a very exhausted wife. At home, his wife Rivkah was finding raising their children to be a challenging task, especially since their young baby had colic and she faced many sleepless nights alone without Michael's help. Usually, by the time Michael came home, Rivkah was worn out and needed assistance. However, when Michael would open the door, his children would crowd around him, start jumping up and down and beg for him to play with them. But Michael who usually felt overwhelmed, would get upset and start leashing out at his kids and yelling at his wife.

To make the situation worse, Rivkah would hand the kids to Michael and run to the bedroom to relax. In response, Michael would turn on the video machine for the children and try to escape to his computer in the living room. Left alone, the children would feel abandoned and start crying for attention, which would cause Michael to lose his temper.

Their situation needed mediation. To resolve this issue they would first need to become aware of their stressors (like work and child-rearing pressures), and then find ways to reduce the stress of the early-evening-bedtime drama. I also suggested that a good place to start would be to repair any emotional damage their arguing would cause by saying they were sorry and admitting that they are overwhelmed.

Michael and Rivkah were relieved to know that there was a way to deal with their problems. Both could learn skills that would help them improve their relationship. They didn't need to be perfect. The true test of their marriage would be if they could learn how to say "I'm sorry."

Saying you're sorry can be difficult, especially if it means admitting you were wrong in the first place. No one likes exposing their imperfections to others, even to those who are very close to them. Admitting you are wrong takes courage. Yet, by using these two simple words, people can make a major difference in their marriage.

First Aid Relationship Tips

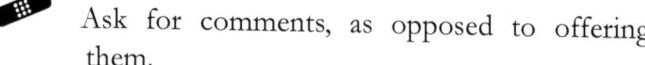 Ask for comments, as opposed to offering them.

Show sincere interest in your spouse when he or she is speaking.

Empathize with them.

Reduce criticism and negative comments.

Use more loving and positive words when you communicate. Actively listen to your spouse's inner messages.

Avoid judging or playing the role of psychologist.

Learn when it's best not to force the issue.

First Aid Exercise 4: Communicating Your Needs

Take a piece of paper. On one half list three things you need from your partner.

On the other half list three things you think your partner needs from you.

Then, have your spouse add in their needs and what they think you need from them. Discuss your findings.

First Aid Exercise 5: Communicating Feelings In Common Situations: "How Do I Feel When..?"

Taking turns, each spouse should reflect on one after another of the 25 questions, and answer what his or her feelings might be in the situation concerned. Either or both of them can answer each question, one after the other, or they can switch back and forth answering only alternate questions.

The purpose of the exercise is to communicate to each other his or her feelings in a certain situation. If each has responded only to alternate questions, and the experience has been a helpful one, they may repeat the exercise, each now answering the question to which only the other had previously responded.

How Do I Feel When…?

You surprise me with something nice.

You show me that you appreciate me.

I make a mistake and you point it out.

You praise or compliment me.

I think that you are judging me.

You make a sacrifice for me.

I am reminded that you really love me.

You seem annoyed with me.

I am buying you a gift.

I don't seem able to reach you.

You frown at me.

You are being too hard on yourself.

You smile at me.

You interrupt me in a conversation.

I think I have hurt your feelings.

You are very upset and begin to cry.

You are sick or in pain.

You ask me to help you.

You become very angry with me.

I can't understand what you are asking me to do.

You tell me you are very proud of me.

First Aid Exercise 6: Examining Your Communication System

We often talk about improving a couple's communication, but we do not always define what bad communication is. Here are ten examples of faulty communication:

1. Avoiding conflict: Hostility builds beneath the surface.

2. Hidden messages: Veiled comments or requests (insinuation) may get the message over, but often cause resentment.

3. Using another family member as a go-between: This creates destructive triangles in the family.

4. Getting family news secondhand: This is a sure indication that there is something wrong with the system.

5. Withholding important information: This creates a vacuum and opens up the way for fantasy, guesswork, or self-blame.

6. Avoiding sensitive areas: Examples are death, money, sex, religion, drugs, alcohol and family skeletons-in-the-closet. The result is misunderstanding, guesswork, and the perpetuation of ignorance.

7. Lying – about anything: This always tends to shake trust and erect barriers.

8. Superficial listening: It is always best to give a straight message, even if it has to be, "I do not have time right now, but let's talk about it later."

9. A closed attitude: This is a put-down, because it means you are not interested in the opinions or concerns of another family member.

10. Refusing to respond or make the first move: This creates a barrier which can harden into alienation.

You might like to check your communication patterns under these ten headings, and see if you can find room for improvement.

First Aid Exercise 7: Tips To Become A Better Listener

Stop Talking!

1) Concentrate – keep the focus on the speaker.

2) Look at the other person.

3) Empathize with the other person; try to understand what is really being said and felt.

4) Reflect to the speaker what has just been said or what you think was just said.

5) Ask non-threatening, open-ended questions.

6) Appropriately communicate non-verbally.

7) Be aware of your emotions and prejudices.

8) Control your anger (or any other emotion which may be keeping you from listening).

9) Get rid of distractions.

10) Get the main points.

11) Share the responsibility for communication.

12) React to ideas, not the person.

13) Don't argue mentally.

14) Listen for what is not said.

---

15) Listen to how something is said.

16) Don't antagonize the speaker.

17) Allow the speaker to speak until she or he has completed their train of thought.

18) Avoid classifying the speaker.

19) Avoid jumping to conclusions.

Go through these individually. Choose those where you think you do well and those where you need to improve. Get together with your spouse and discuss your choices on each of these points. Have your choices been similar? Different?

CHAPTER 4
REDUCING CONTROLLING
BEHAVIOR

In This Chapter:

- The dangers of controlling and abusive behavior

- How controlling behavior starts

- How to recognize control in marriage

- Marriage care: working together

Controlling behavior may be the number one reason that your marriage needs first aid.

If you are unfamiliar with the topic of control, it's no surprise. Most people are unaware that control is a major topic for counselors, therapists and psychologists-at-large, which until recently has not entered into the public's attention.

Now many counselors are beginning to talk about control, including one of the leading Orthodox experts on marriage and relationships, Rabbi Abraham J. Twerski, M.D., who wrote an entire book on the topic. In "Successful Relationships: At Home, at Work, and with Friends: Bringing Control Issues Under Control," Rabbi Twerski explains that, "Everyone may have the need to wield control, and there are many relationships which may indeed require control. Exceeding an acceptable amount of control invites trouble."

Trouble, indeed. Think about your relationships. Which ones do you find meaningful and enjoyable and which ones do you avoid like the plague? Take your friends, for example. Do you try to control them, tell them what to do, yell at them, kvetch when you don't get what you want right away? Probably not. So why do we feel free to try to control our closest and most intimate relationships? Perhaps this is due to human nature taking over. When we are married and live with someone for many years, we get accustomed to their habits; we get used to their small idiosyncrasies and begin to take for granted that, on some level, they exist to fulfill our needs.

Did you ever wonder why people who have been married for 20, 30 or more years can claim that they love each other but are always yelling at one another? I see these kinds of couples all the time, and not just in my office. Last summer I took my children to an amusement park and had to wait in lines for hours under the hot August heat. Standing next to me was a couple who must have been in their late 40s, with four children around ages 17, 13, 12, and 8. They all seemed on edge and upset about standing in line, with hundreds of people in front of them waiting to take a 90-second plunge down the latest monster roller coaster. Their conversation went something like this:

Husband (to wife): I am getting so tired standing here!

Wife (to husband): I told you about the long lines.

Husband: Why can't they make this go quicker?

Wife: There you go again, blaming everybody.

Husband: Blaming? That's your job around here. You are so hot-tempered today, I 'm losing my cool.

Wife (trying to hush him down while everybody was listening to their little fight): Okay; I can't stand it when you berate me in public!

At this point their twelve-year-old and eight-year-old children started pushing each other and the younger one started crying. And then, the mother started yelling at her oldest son to behave better, and the father turned around and screamed, "Cut it out or go home!"

This all points to the fact, that deep down inside, people believe that they somehow can control each other's behavior. In this family, for example, the father thought that he could control the people waiting in line and started complaining out loud. His wife thought she could control her husband's outbursts by putting him down, and by doing so, defuse his behavior. The husband then tried controlling her and started ranting and raving about her negative attitude. And once again, the wife tried controlling her whole family so that they wouldn't look silly in front of the other customers.

You'll notice from this family that the need for control is often circular; first you try to control someone, then in response, they try to control you back. That makes you even angrier and intensifies your desire to gain even more control in the relationship.

That's why as a counselor, I often find myself teaching couples how to moderate their level of control and increase their levels of mutual respect. The line of reasoning flows like this:

Less control and more focus on the relationship = healthy marriages.

More control and less focus on the relationship = unhealthy marriages.

When people are less controlling in marriage they are a lot more pleasant to be around. They also find it easier to create loving and supportive relationships. Living with a high controller is much more difficult. They tend to create emotional distance and the people living with them develop the following beliefs about themselves:

- They are stuck with another person's definition of them.

- They do not have the right to their own opinions.

- They can earn love and acceptance by abdicating control to another person.

- They are "successful" if they fulfill another person's vision, even when it does not in any way support their own.

- They must obtain permission to act in matters that are, in fact, their own business.

There is no doubt that control breeds hostility and resentment. Take Meir, 32, and Sarah, 30, a couple that tried to control every aspect of each other's lives. Meir had decided (without negotiating this with his wife) how Sarah should raise their children, where she should shop, how much money she should spend, and whether or not she should have a cell phone. As a case in point, Meir thought that Sarah was overly permissive with their children and spent too much time reading to them at night. Feeling it was his "right" to correct her behavior, Meir would insult Sarah about her parenting skills — sometimes in private, and at other times in front of their children. He would berate her endlessly about the times their children acted out, and how everything was due to her "poor parenting skills."

Sarah was enraged that Meir was exposing her and their children to his belittling and degrading comments. In sheer desperation, she began her own form of controlling behavior by going on shopping sprees and spending money beyond their means. Before they knew it, Sarah had racked up over seven-thousand dollars on their VISA bill, believing that she could spend as much money as she wanted despite the devastating consequences to her family.

It was pretty easy for me to see that her shopping habits were directly connected to how her husband was treating her at home. The more harshly he behaved with her, the bigger the VISA bill. Sarah was trying to control her husband by hitting him with unsuspecting bills that would inevitably drive him crazy.

As usual, the circle of control didn't stop there. Meir kept complaining about Sarah's parenting skills and eventually decided to further control Sarah by cutting off her VISA card. He also felt that she could not be trusted to spend money as she pleased and opened up his own bank account without consulting her.

What really pushed Sarah over the edge was when Meir started reading her cell phone bills and questioning why she was calling her friends during the day (which would cost more minutes than their monthly family plan would allow).

Their marriage was in a shambles and with the friction burning in their home, their relationship was in serious crisis.

Marriages like this are not uncommon. When a spouse yields an inordinate amount of control over areas such as finances, education, food and vacation plans while leaving their spouse totally in the dark, the results can be catastrophic.

And it's not just about controlling behavior, but attitude and perspective as well. A controlling personality tends to ignore his or her spouses needs and focuses only on what they view as necessary to maintain their own sense of security and equilibrium. The controller's message is: It's my way or the highway!

There's no doubt that control problems also affect a multitude of family relationships, especially those with children and teenagers. Take David, 42, and Lisa, 38, for example. They came together with their two teenage boys, Daniel, 15, and Gavriel, 13, to discuss Daniel's at-risk behavior.

The situation in their home had become unbearable. The previous Shabbos, Daniel got in a fist fight with his younger brother and ended up breaking a window in their bedroom. This was not their first fight, but one of their worst ones in years. David and Lisa had also brought with them a laundry list of complaints about Daniel's behavior. They felt that he wasn't taking school seriously, that he was fighting in class, and worst of all, he was consistently rude to his parents.

To make matters worse, David started blaming Lisa for Daniel's problems. He believed that she was "too accepting," "parented without borders," and "never disciplined him for doing wrong." The tension in the room quickly boiled over and Daniel and Lisa started snapping at and insulting one another.

After calming down the situation, I began searching for clues to Daniel's behavior. Was he a victim of abuse from one of his teachers? Did he suffer from a learning disability? Did he have an attention deficit?

I believed that the clues to their son's at-risk behavior weren't to be found "out on the street," or in Daniel's school. The source of their problem was sitting right in their room with us. It was obvious that Daniel's father, David, had a controlling personality and difficulty managing his anger. And now Daniel had learned how to control others through attacking those who disagreed with him. Daniel was simply mirroring the at-risk behavior he had learned from his father at home.

To help this family, I aimed to reduce their use of external control. They needed to stop insulting one another and instead treat each other with respect. David was a "controller," and the results, on an emotional level, were disastrous.

The lesson for marriage is that if we expect to be treated in a fair and loving manner, we need to be careful how we exercise control in our closest relationships. We also need to become sensitive to our spouse's needs, and first and foremost, develop an attitude of respect for one another.

Let me illustrate this point with the story of a couple who were dealing with control issues. About two years ago a woman named Bracha, 47, came to speak to me about her husband's controlling behavior. This is how she described her precarious situation to me:

"My husband is a very controlling person. He likes to be in charge of everything and he's always telling me what to do. It's driving me crazy. I feel like I can't live up to his standards. He's critical about almost everything I do, like my housework, taking care of the kids, and how I talk in front of his friends. When I clean the house, he quizzes me on what I had accomplished, how long it took and how to improve in the future. I tend to lean toward perfectionism, so you can imagine how frustrating it is for me to spend hours trying to meet his needs and then have him question me on my behavior!."

There was no question that Bracha was suffering from an overly controlling husband. Instead of respecting and caring for his wife, he chose to belittle and berate her for not living up to his unrealistic demands. Worse, Bracha had tried her best to please her husband and was now made to feel that she was a failure and would be treated as a second-class citizen.

For those who find it difficult to imagine this extreme behavior, try to remember the last time you felt controlled by someone close to you, and then multiply that feeling by one-hundred-fold. Most of us have experienced some kind of control in our lives. For example, your parents may have tried to control what you ate or when you went to sleep. At work, you may have experienced a boss who aimed to control your behavior or ensure that your productivity was high. In the classroom, your teachers may have tried to control your behavior and make sure you focused on your studies.

Some people grew up in families where anger and criticism were used as methods to control each other. If these external forms of control were used in your family, you may have learned to respond to it with compliance: being a good girl or boy. You may have learned to put aside your own feelings and go along with what others wanted, in the hope of avoiding their wrath.

After learning how to handle control as a child, some utilize the same principles in marriage. Now it manifests itself in a new way, for example, trying to "baby" your spouse by controlling his or her every move, giving in easily to what they want, or retreating or resisting their attempts to control you, are all systems of control.

The following story illustrates how control can destroy a marriage. Eliyahu, 38, and Shaina, 35, started counseling when they were on the verge of divorce. After 12 years of marriage, their relationship was deteriorating and they were quickly drifting apart.

The following is from a transcript of one of our sessions:

Eliyahu: I guess I feel that Shaina is just so distant and unaffectionate. Most of the time she's critical and I can't seem to do anything right in her eyes. I try really hard to please her, but no matter what I do, it's not good enough. I want her to appreciate me and say "thank you," for what I do give to her. I wish she would be warmer with me and let me know that she still loves me.

Daniel Schonbuch (DS): Shaina, Eliyahu feels that you are distant and don't appreciate who he is or what he does.

Shaina: Don't appreciate him? I just can't seem to connect with him anymore. I feel irritated around him and I don't really know why. He just annoys me. I feel like he's clingy and I don't like being around him.

DS: You said you don't know why you dislike like him. Is there anything specific that you can point to?

Shaina: Well, for one thing, he doesn't appreciate how hard I work for him. I work in a high-pressured accounting office and often come home late. When I do, he seems irritated and usually attacks me by saying that our kids are burdening him. But, you know, I work too hard for him to complain. I spend too many hours slaving at work for him to complain about me! I wish he would get a better job so I could stop working so hard! But he's such a failure in business and I can't stand having to bear the burden for the entire family.

Despite Eliyahu's attempts to move closer to his wife, every possible advance was being rejected by Shaina, who would stonewall or retreat into her own emotional world.

In this marriage, Eliyahu was acting like a caretaker. He tried to control her by being a "nice guy" and doing everything he thought Shaina wanted, including making dinner every night, doing the laundry, and taking care of his children. He secretly believed that if he was kind enough, he could control Shaina's love for him. What he didn't realize is that his niceness was really a "pull" on Shaina, which is one reason she kept her distance. Underneath, Eliyahu had a big fear of rejection and was trying to have control over Shaina not rejecting him.

On the other hand, Shaina was trying to control Eliyahu, primarily with her criticism. She was critical any time she felt Eliyahu wanted something from her that would make him feel safe and loved. She had a secret hope that if she criticized him enough, he would stop pulling on her for affection and attention. Unconsciously, Shaina had a huge fear of being "swallowed up" and was trying to protect herself from being controlled by Eliyahu. Shaina could not experience who Eliyahu was because he was putting himself aside to please her. She could not connect with him until he was authentically himself. The more Eliyahu pulled with niceness, the more Shaina moved away, and the more Shaina moved away, the more Eliyahu pulled.

Both Eliyahu and Shaina needed to learn how to take loving care of themselves, rather than attempt to control the other. Eliyahu needed to learn how to not take Shaina's behavior as a personal rejection. He needed to see that her withdrawal was coming from her fear of engulfment that he was tapping into, but he was not the cause of her fear. She had this fear way before meeting him. Eliyahu also needed to start to be loving to himself rather than "nice" to Shaina. He needed to learn to take responsibility for his own feelings of well-being, instead of being dependent upon Shaina for them. In learning to take care of himself, he would naturally stop pulling on Shaina for his sense of worth and security.

I suggested to Shaina that she needed to moderate the tone of her comments and needed to learn to speak her truth without blaming or judging. She could say things like, "Eliyahu, I appreciate the dinner you made, but I feel like you made it with an expectation that I should now love you, rather than because you felt like making dinner. I'd rather that you not make dinner unless you are doing it because you really want to, and without an expectation attached. I feel pulled-on and it doesn't feel good."

Eliyahu and Shaina decided that it was worth learning how to give love to themselves, and then see what happened with their marriage. Fortunately, because both of them were devoted to learning to take full, 100% responsibility for their own feelings and needs, they were able to move out of their protective, controlling circle and into a loving circle. As they learned to take responsibility for themselves, their love for each other gradually returned.

In a healthy marriage, control is at bare minimum; both individuals develop a sense of mutuality and respect, carrying out their different duties and roles. When they need to "talk out" issues they do so in a kind and compassionate manner. When they disagree, they are able to resolve their disagreements and move on with their marriage and relationship.

How Controlling Behavior Starts

Control is not usually a major factor at the beginning of marriage, when most people start off by putting their best foot forward and limiting excessive behavior. In most dating situations it would be highly unlikely to see a young man rant and rave if his first-time shidduch is five minutes late for a date. Both sides are still in an illusionary phase of the relationship, where they are careful to limit any form of criticism and to maintain an air of civility during all interchanges.

During the initial phase of the relationship people tend to treat their fiancé as a friend. However, over time, controlling behaviors can silently creep in and become apparent when one side starts to yield an imbalance of power over the other. They also start objectifying the other person and mistakenly believe that they were created to serve their needs. And, when they don't get their way, they feel it's their right to force them to comply and do what they want.

It is true that you may think that what you want should be acceptable to your spouse, when in truth it is debasing or demeaning. Of course there are many circumstances that demand we do things that we don't feel are easy or pleasant. For instance, a parent finds it hard to tell their child to behave in a certain way. A wife or husband may complain that they need more help around the house or with their children. The problem begins when we start believing that we can actually control the other person's behavior, and we don't have to negotiate for what we need.

In counseling I often see situations where a husband is giving to his wife all the things that he "thinks" she wants. He may buy for his wife every imaginable comfort including a beautiful home, car, clothing etc. Yet, she may feel that her husband is emotionally detached and unresponsive to the things she really wants like warmth and affection.

Meir, 24 and Tzipporah, 22, were recently married and were each feeling that the other was unresponsive to his/her needs. Although the relationship started out with both individuals respecting one another, over the last few months, Tzipporah had begun to feel that her husband was wielding too much control over their finances. About two months prior to their first visit, without Tzipporah's knowledge, Meir had decided to open up his own bank account and that he would be solely responsible for their finances. Tzipporah would not have direct access to money, and instead would be given a small "allowance" for spending each week.

Clearly, Meir had begun to control his wife, by using money as his primary weapon. I was interested in exploring if money was the only area of control in their lives. Often, control starts out in other areas, such as emotional control, or control over how love is shared or reserved to punish the other person. This is, it turned out, how Meir had shown early signs of controlling behavior. During their dating period, Meir began to take unusual control over their relationship. At first, he would insist on deciding when and where they would dine. At first, she viewed this behavior as somewhat gallant or chivalrous, and at a certain level she even enjoyed it, because she thought there was something charmingly old-fashioned about it.

However, one night, he ordered her a dish that she knew she really would not like, and when she tried to chime in to tell the waiter to get her something else instead, he glared at her until she felt shamed into silence.

During that date, Tzipporah found herself fuming inside throughout the rest of the dinner, all the while trying her hardest to conceal her anger at his having treated her like a child in front of their waiter. Through a sheer act of will, she managed to keep up a steady patter of superficial, meaningless small talk, but she barely touched her meal. (After all, it was something she did not like.) She wanted to speak up afterward, when they were finally alone together in the car, but for some strange reason, she found that she was almost afraid to do so. It was a strange, unfamiliar feeling, being somewhat fearful and on guard around the person whom she believed she loved, and who, likewise, claimed to love her.

So, rather than directly confronting him about how his actions had made her feel, the following day she called her sister to talk about it. She was initially embarrassed to tell her sister what had transpired, and she wasn't even sure which aspect of the situation was the greatest source of her embarrassment:

the fact that her fiancé had treated her like a child in front of that waiter, or the fact that she had felt afraid — genuinely afraid — of confronting him about how badly he had behaved.

Once she finally forced herself to get the words out, about exactly what had happened, and how awful she had felt about it afterward, her sister asked (just as any concerned sister would), "Is he always this controlling?"

At first, she felt dumbstruck. It was never something she had really thought about, at least not in those precise terms. She knew Meir was a bit of a "stickler" about certain things, but she figured that we all have our little foibles, and up until now, she had never really envisioned that this side of his personality could actually be emotionally destructive in any way.

But now she felt compelled to re-examine everything that had gone on during their relationship in a new light. And when she did start to think more deeply about his behavior, it slowly started to dawn on her that all of the little bossy, nit-picky things that he did, and all of the odd little "rules and regulations" that he had always insisted upon, might actually add up to an excessively controlling personality.

Relationship Test

Understanding Meir and Tzipporah's marriage can help others spot signs of controlling behavior in their relationships. Here are some of the ways to know whether you are in a controlling relationship:

1) Does your spouse want you to themselves all of the time?

Your relationship is fresh and new, both of you are into each others, and your spouse may be what is called "relationship-centered," which means they value and put all of their energy into relationships before any of their other values such as work or friends. There is nothing wrong with being relationship-centered, but where the line between relationship-centered and controlling occurs, is when your spouse is not interested in your going out with your friends at all, or is not interested in letting you have time to yourself. If you do go out with others or spend time by yourself, they will complain and you will never hear the end of it; you will often feel like they are trying to make you feel guilty or bad for leaving them alone. If you begin to feel like it is easier to just drop the amount of times you see your friends and family, in order to prevent the constant complaining from your spouse, this may be an indication that their attempts at controlling you may be working. You will also find family and friends saying things to you like, "Where have you disappeared to?", "I don't see you anymore," or "Did you drop off the face of the earth?"

2) Does your spouse complain to, or is he or she rude to your family and friends?

It may be fine at first when you, your spouse, your friends and/or family get together, but over time, as your relationship continues, if your spouse starts becoming rude to your family and friends to a point where it is uncomfortable for you, and your spouse complains before and after they get together with your friends and family, this may be another indication of your spouse being controlling as well. He or she may be trying to influence you to stop getting together with your friends and family, or they may be trying to make it so uncomfortable when all of you get together, that you start seeing your friends and family without your spouse.

3) Does your spouse try to give you suggestions on how to change yourself?

In the beginning of the relationship, you may have tried changing aspects of yourself to ensure that your spouse likes you, but now you have begun to notice that your spouse is constantly giving you suggestions on how to talk, act, what to wear and what to do. If your spouse is making these types of suggestions, this is also an indication that your spouse is into control or trying to change you, versus just allowing and loving you just the way you are.

4) Do you have to repeat yourself several times before your spouse listens to you?

Some personalities are more naturally dominant than others. They are natural leaders, like to be in charge, and are into completing tasks, but they are not into people, and are solely interested in getting from point A to point B. They often get mistaken as being controlling, and often will tune people out when they are trying to get something completed. Often they are not aware that they come across as controlling at home, because their style usually works for them in their workplace.

However, the difference between someone who is a natural leader and someone who is intentionally controlling is that a leader will make an attempt to learn how to communicate and negotiate with their spouse, out of fairness. But a person who is controlling is not interested in learning communication or negotiation. They are only interested in doing what they want in the way they want to.

5) Does your spouse use controlling language like "you should," or "I insist"?

Most people don't realize that they can be controlling without knowing. Almost all of us use certain language and phrases that give orders directly to our subconscious mind without knowing we are doing it. Whenever we use the phrase, "You should," we are influencing others, since "you should," is a directive statement. Then other people may have been taught, often by society and their own upbringing, that they can control others by using guilt or social influence, by saying things like, "What would your parents think if you didn't give me a ride?" or, "What would your friends think if you didn't get them an expensive gift?" The difference between someone who is just using these words or terminology and someone who is intentionally trying to use these forms of influence is that every second sentence coming out of the controlling person is a controlling phrase. In addition, if your spouse is putting a lot of emotion into their controlling phrases and sentences, you may have someone who is too controlling in your life.

To achieve real and lasting love, each person needs to shift from direct control, and focus on altruistically fulfilling the other's stated needs. In a healthy relationship, each side senses that control is never a solution, whereas mutual respect and recognition are the only ways toward living beyond the moment.

Finally, there are marriages where either spouse may find themselves in a physically or emotionally abusive relationship. If abuse is present, one or both of the spouses needs to seek professional help. As a first step, I suggest a call to a domestic abuse hotline like Shalom Task Force at 1-888-883-2323. They specialize in dealing with abuse in the Jewish community and are sensitive to the needs of Orthodox Jews. Their confidential hotline offers a listening ear and referrals to key community agencies that can assist victims. Their website www.

shalomtaskforce.org is filled with insightful articles and information about domestic abuse and what to do if you think you are being abused.

First Aid Relationship Tips

 Shift from direct control to mutual understanding.

 Limit controlling behavior.

 Avoid confrontation.

 Be sensitive to your spouse's inner world.

First Aid Exercise 8: Marriage Care: Working Together

Think about a project the two of you worked on that stands out in your memory (something baked, built, made, presented, etc.). Why do you remember this event? How were your different approaches evident as you worked together?

Did you delight in the other, or disagree on how to do it?

Are there any things you would like to ask your spouse to change (in regard to working together) if he or she could?

What do you appreciate the most about your spouse when working on something together?

How do you see that you can complement each other in your future life together, your work, and your home?

First Aid Exercise 9: Domestic Abuse Checklist

Below are just some of the signs that you may be in an abusive relationship. For more information, contact Shalom Task Force hotline at 1-888-883-2323.

Frequently blames or criticizes you

Calls you names

Criticizes or threatens to hurt your family or friends

Isolates you from your family and friends

Becomes angry if meals or housework are not done to his/her liking

Repeatedly harasses you about things you did in the past

Takes away car keys, money or credit cards

Threatens to leave or told you to leave.

Checks up on you (listens to your phone calls, looks at phone bills, checks the mileage on the car, etc.)

Takes care of all financial matters without your input

Forces you to provide marital relations against your will

Pushes, grabs, slaps, punches kicks or shoves you

CHAPTER 5
CONFLICT RESOLUTION

In this chapter:

• Principles for conflict resolution

• Compromise and commitment

• A good basis for marriage

No matter how couples try to make sure everything is perfect in their lives, at some point they may experience conflict in their marriage. Conflict is not as dramatic as it sounds. In marriage, independent of how much you love someone, you may have differing ideas about money or education, preferences, or various special activities you both want to do. Learning how to resolve these differences, appropriately, can avoid prolonged or destructive anger and hostility. Conflict resolution skills include cultivating the right attitude as well as learning interpersonal techniques.

To begin with, most arguments on some level stem from misunderstanding. One spouse might perceive the other's action or inaction or words as being very unreasonable and most inappropriate in a given circumstance. People are quick to take their positions and justify their stand rather than to try to understand the other party. Added to this problem of misunderstanding are feelings of pride where people put up a bold front and avoid giving in to their spouse. In some marriages, a small war might rage for days before the conflict is resolved and in between, tension and unhappiness builds.

Take Rachel 27, and David, 28 who came to speak to me about a fight they were having over raising their eight year old son, Yosef. Yosef was by all means a rambunctious third grader who kept his teacher and parents hopping on their toes day and night. Rachel who had two other young children in their home was finding raising them together with Yosef's ADD-like behavior overwhelming. She was also upset that her husband, David, came home late from work and wasn't pulling his weight around the house. The home-related stress was causing conflict and Rachel and David were unable to resolve their problems peacefully.

Understanding Differences in Communication

It is true that many couples like Rachel and David face similar stress-filled situations, yet are able to maintain a positive relationship. The difference between Rachel and David and others, is the *way* they argue and the defensive styles of communication they maintain. Rachel, for example, tends to be very assertive. She's quick to blame David for the stress that she's feeling at home and berates him the second he enters the door until the minute they go to sleep. David on the other hand is an "avoider" who shies away from conflict. He has more of an easy-go-lucky personality and hushes up like an obedient puppy when his wife yells at him. Together, the mixture of Rachel's competitive style and David's avoidance of conflict has created a relationship that was low on trust and high on negative feelings.

One way for Rachel and David to deal with their conflict is through them becoming aware of their negative styles of communication. According to family therapists there are several key styles of communication that people develop: competitive, avoidant, and compromising.

Competitive Style

When a person uses a competitive style, they tend to be very assertive and interested in getting their own way. They also approach the conflict in a forceful manner without being interested in cooperating with other people and view their relationship from a win/lose perspective.

People use the competitive style when an issue is very important to them. Or when the person has the authority to make the decision, and it seems clear that this is the one best way. They can also become competitive when decisions have to be made fast and the person has power to make it as the following dialogue shows:

Moshe (irritated): You didn't turn off the lights in the bathroom when you were finished. How many times do I have to remind you?

Shani (sarcastic tone): Why do you have to make such a big deal about a few cents worth of electricity?

Moshe (harshly): Because you're irresponsible about money, that's why!

Shani (reacting): Maybe you'd save more money if I just moved out.

When someone is competitive, they look upon a family discussion or disagreement as being sort of like a debate or contest.

In a contest, it's natural for humans to want to score more points than their opponent.

When spouses seek to score points against one another, a family discussion quickly degenerates into a win/lose competition. As disagreement heats up, spouses begin using increasingly abusive comments to "score points."

Usually these hurtful words do not express what the two spouses really feel about each other. They're just caught up in the heat of competition. When the dust settles both spouses wonder how the mess got started in the first place and wish they could take back the words they said. Unfortunately, the "winner" settles down in a cloud of gloom and thinks, "Boy, I won that one! Soooo... how come I feel so bad?"

Avoidant Style

This approach happens when a person does not assert himself, doesn't know how to cooperate or wants to avoid conflict entirely. Although this can temporarily be a good approach to use if one is dealing with a difficult person, in the long run, it leaves issues unresolved and can linger on far beyond the event. Avoidance can mean to others that a person is 'running away' from them and they feel they can take advantage of the situation. Their inner message is that they need to maintain a lose/win attitude to survive.

The avoider on the outside may seem to give in, but at the same time, they can build considerable resentment towards their spouse for denying their feelings and agreeing to things they feel are wrong or hurtful.

When one partner always retreats from difficult discussions, the other partner pushes even harder to achieve a resolution. As the pusher pushes harder, the retreater retreats further. Eventually the distance between spouses can become an uncrossable chasm.

Compromising Style

A compromiser is a person who maintains the principle of win/win in their marriage. In the compromising approach, one gives up a little of what he wants to get the rest of what he wants and the other party is also willing to do the same. This is done by making exchanges, concessions and bargaining to come up with a compromise solution both parties agree to.

The idea of winning, where the opponent loses, can work in games like chess or basketball, but not in marriage. When you are connected to someone (in marriage, or other close relationships), if you "win," and they "lose," you'll lose as well, in the long run.

A win-win approach looks for solutions that please and work for both of you. If your heart's dream is to take a vacation and your spouse's dream is to renovate the kitchen you may need to work hard to come up with a win-win solution. Possibilities might be to have a short vacation this winter, and next year, invest in your kitchen.

Towards a Higher Level of Communication

In evaluating these three styles, being competitive or avoiding conflict share the same risk of alienating the other person. A competitive person tends to blame their spouse for their feelings and denies taking responsibility for their own actions. It's always the *other* person's fault for what is going wrong in their lives. The avoider, however, has the opposite problem, it's always their own fault and they feel responsible for everything that goes wrong in the relationship.

The third style, to compromise, creates a foundation for a successful marriage. Once you are able to wield it effectively, it can make the difference between an average relationship and one that the world will admire. It won't be easy. Anything that is worth doing is hard and takes work. Compromise is a part of daily life, after all. To make it work for you and your relationship, there needs to be an open channel of communication. This will allow you to understand how compromise affects you both. If you can do that, you can use it to power your relationship far beyond the bounds of normal play and end up with marriage where the whole is greater than the sum of its parts.

In any relationship, compromise means give and take, and it's a part of daily life for all couples. You may be the talkative one in a relationship, but conversation with your spouse should be 50/50. For example, you may want to spend your *yom tov* with your parents or c*hol hamoed* with your in-laws, but a bit of both is what makes a relationship work. Compromise is allowing for things to get in the way of your ideal daily life for the sake of your relationship. What may seem like a disadvantage at first quickly changes into one of the greatest advantages of your life when you realize that from compromise comes the base of your relationship.

The best way to embrace and understand compromise in your relationship is to talk about it. An open dialogue is important for both parties. Keeping your feelings bottled up doesn't do anyone any good. The lines of communication need to be open. You need to share how you feel about the compromises you both are making for the sake of your relationship. Find out how they feel about their position and try and understand the need for balance and fairness. In the end, compromise usually means that you win some and you lose some but you both get to come out ahead together.

How does a person move towards cooperation and avoid maintaining either a competitive or avoidance style of communication? In order for effective communication and conflict resolution to occur, there must be an understanding about rules that will facilitate or impair the process. Here are some of the principles that couples can use to reduce conflict in their marriage:

1. Try to take a problem-solving attitude toward issues, versus one of blame. Problem solving is much more practical and leads people in a different—and more productive—direction than blame. Assigning responsibility is useful, to the degree it helps to generate solutions. But blame has a component of *punishment* attached.

2. Learn to take a "time out," in order to cool your anger until you're able to be responsible for your behavior. A time out can be used to do things that allow you to gain self-control and to mellow out. You could exercise (walk, jog, bicycle), do relaxation exercises, stretching, or yoga, or say *tehilim*.

3. Make use of "cool down" activities—less formal than time outs, *cool downs* can be momentary breaks that allow both of you to catch your breath and de-escalate. You could offer to make a cup of tea or coffee, or a sandwich. You could propose a walk around the block. You could suggest, "Hey, let's stop and take a deep breath." Or say, "I'm feeling pretty tense. Give me a moment here. How about if I get both of us something to drink, so I can calm down, and we can continue to have a good discussion?" It usually doesn't work if you say, "Hey, calm down!" You're actions are likely to be perceived as a put-down and an attempt to control the other person's behavior.

In some cases however, compromise may not be possible. That may be due to the fact that beyond communication styles exist another level hiding behind the surface. When you look beyond "why" people are arguing you can often uncover "what" they are really arguing about. For example, a wife is very picky about the types of birthday presents her husband buys for her. She never seems happy about her gifts and leaves her husband feeling that he is inferior. One possibility is that she has an outstanding artistic sense and expects that every piece of jewelry fit in perfectly with her collection. Another possibility is that she feels her husband is not affectionate enough and is really looking for more love.

Take Meir, 45, and Leah, 44, for example. They came to resolve their complaint that neither was fully "engaged" in their marriage. Meir was a successful lawyer who worked long and hard hours at his firm. He believed that he was a good husband who provided for his wife's every need. They had a large house, several cars, went away twice a year on exotic vacations etc. Meir also described himself as an "avoider" and his wife as being confrontational. Leah, on the other hand was busy running their children's school's PTA, studying towards a second degree in Art Therapy and taking courses in their local shul. In short, Meir and Leah never saw each other, but when they did, they were always fighting about money, Meir's "sloppiness" and how to renovate their home.

At first, I tried to work through their conflict under the assumption that Meir was avoiding his wife, and Leah was too confrontational. After several sessions I saw that we weren't making any headway and I decided to probe even deeper. It turned out that the *real* problem in their marriage was the lack of affection that was caused by their inability to spend quality time together. Each was living as a separate entity under the same roof. They lacked the aspect of "dodi", and were missing the closeness needed to sustain a happy marriage. For Meir and Leah marriage turned into a business deal, an agreement where each side did the minimal amount needed to continue the relationship while sharing no real joy or excitement about one another.

Meir and Leah were not just fighting about matching pastel colors or the size of their chandeliers. They were fighting about the loneliness in their marriage and using the walls of their home as their battle ground.

When people argue endlessly about the same topics it is a sign that they are really talking about something much deeper. There may even exist unsolvable problems and differences that pop up as conflict over money, education or work stress. In reality, their problems can't be solved through changing their style of communication. Couples who can't break their vitriolic patterns need to discover their deeper wishes and desires that are unfulfilled or being denied by their spouse.

Some of a person's deeper wishes may include:

- Wanting more love and affection

- Desiring greater control in their lives

- Getting respect from people

- Wanting to feel secure about their relationship

- Desire to live a long life

- Financial security

- Overcoming past hurts i.e. Divorced parents, death in family, loss of money, failure

Often it is these wishes that fuel unresolved conflicts. For example, arguing over raising children may be more than just a fight about changing diapers. The daily stress of attending to a child's needs may be exacerbated by a wish that their child will succeed in school or that they will become a doctor, lawyer or wealthy businessman. Or, for parents of a child who tends to act out, the may harbor a deep-seated wish that their child will be perfect and never struggle or compromise their values. Sometimes you find couples arguing endlessly about their in-laws, when in actuality they are upset about the lack of affection in their marriage.

If you are arguing in circles about the same issues its crucial to define your hidden expectations and overall goals for your marriage.

Let's begin by looking at a hypothetical story of Yaakov that teaches a valuable lesson on the problems of "hidden goals."

Yaakov is a young businessman, just starting out in business. Although he has a very tight budget, Yaakov knows he needs a computer for his work.

Yaakov visits a computer retail store. When the salesperson asks Yaakov how he will use the computer, Yaakov answers, "Just simple stuff. I want something that's inexpensive."

Yaakov buys a basic, low-priced computer. Then, over the Internet, Yaakov buys a powerful Computer Automated Design (CAD) program. To his dismay, Yaakov quickly learns that his cheap computer is unable to run the CAD program. When Yaakov returns to the computer store he discovers that upgrading his low-end computer to do CAD will cost him a bundle. The store refuses to take his computer back or give him a trade-in.

When analyzing what went wrong, I believe that Yaakov made at least two mistakes: (1) he didn't clearly reveal his goal to the computer store and (2) his goal of using a cheap computer to do Computer Automated Design was unrealistic.

More often than not, people fail to clearly communicate their goals and wishes to one another and end up arguing about the most mundane things. When you get married you expect certain things of your spouse and your spouse expects certain things of you. Marriages most often get in trouble because spouses fail to meet each other's goals and expectations.

In many cases, spouses fail to meet each other's marital goals for the simple reason that they have not honestly and clearly communicated them to one other. One example is Leah, 27, and Chaim, 28, who were on the verge of divorce when they came to speak with me about their marriage. According to Chaim, they lived on a tight budget in order to put every possible penny into a savings account. As the savings account grew, Chaim dreamed of being able to buy a house. On the other hand, Leah dreamed of returning to college and becoming a nurse. Three years into the marriage, and after the birth of two children, Chaim and Leah were shocked to learn that they were saving money with two altogether different goals in mind.

What went wrong? Notice that neither of their expectations was out-and-out unreasonable. The problem was that their expectations did not match and they never clearly stated and discussed their respective goals. Leah and Chaim never sat down and evaluated their wishes. To avoid conflict, both need to find out more about each other by doing a relationship inventory.

A relationship inventory is designed to get you and your spouse into a clear and productive discussion of your respective goals, expectations, and dreams for the future.

Many couples have found this effort to be extremely beneficial to their relationship.

How to do a Relationship Inventory

1. Print out separate copies of the form for each of you.

2. Each partner should fill out the form independently.

3. The form is not perfect. You may have expectations or goals in other areas. If so, by all means feel free to add items, delete items, and edit the form as you see fit.

4. When completed, exchange forms with each other. After several days, get together and discuss them.

Aid Exercise 10: The Relationship Inventory

A - Parenting

1) Who is responsible for caring for your children?

A) Me b) My spouse c)Both of us

2) Who is responsible for late-night feedings?

a) Me b) My spouse c)Both of us

3) What actions do you feel should be taken if your child develops disciplinary problems?

a) Me b) My spouse c)Both of us

4) Who should have the main responsibility for dealing with your child's serious disciplinary problems?

a) Me b) My spouse c)Both of us

5) Who should usually be expected to take time off from work if your child is ill or has special needs?

a) Me b) My spouse c)Both of us

B - Earning money

6) What job or career do you want to have?_____

7) What would be the extent of your work hours?

a) Full-time b) Part-time c) Only work "now & then," as needed to supplement the family's income

8) If your long-term career goal will require additional education or training during your marriage, please answer the following questions...

a) Approximately how long will be needed for the education or training?_____
b) Approximately how much money will it cost for the education or training?_____
c) During what hours would you obtain this education or training?

Week-days Week-ends Evenings Home study

9) What hours do you expect that your spouse will spend at work?

a) Full-time b) Part-time c) Only work "now & then," as needed to supplement the family's income

10) If your spouse's long-term career goal should ever require extensive additional education or training during your marriage, please answer the following questions...

a) How much of a sacrifice in "family togetherness" are you willing to make?

A little - A lot -As much as necessary

b) How much of a sacrifice in family finances are you willing to make?

A little - A lot -As much as necessary

11) Whose job or career should have top priority in your family?

a) My spouse's b) Mine c) Our jobs should be completely equal

C - Family finances

12) What amount of responsibility should you have for earning money to meet your family's financial needs?

a) Sole responsibility
b) Main responsibility
c) Equal responsibility with my spouse
d) Responsible only for supplemental income
e) No responsibility

13) What amount of responsibility should your spouse have for earning money to meet your family's financial needs?

a) Sole responsibility
b) Main responsibility
c) Equal responsibility with me
d) Responsible only for supplemental income
e) No responsibility

14) Who should have "the final say" on your family's financial decisions?

a) Me b) My spouse c)Both of us

15) Other than for household expenses, should you have a personal checking or savings account separate from your spouse's?

a) Yes b) No c)Both of us

16) What are your main near-term goals for the use of your family's savings?_____

17) What are your main long-term goals for the use of your family's savings?_____

18) Suppose you are given an opportunity to have a big increase in the money you earn. However, this opportunity requires that, for the next 2 to 4 years, you will have to spend extra time working and studying. How much "family time" are you willing to sacrifice for such an opportunity?

a) None
b) 1 to 2 evenings weekly
c) 1 to 2 evenings weekly, plus some weekend days
d) 3 to 4 evenings weekly
e) 3 to 4 evenings weekly, plus some weekend days
f) As much as necessary

19) Suppose your spouse is given an opportunity to have a big increase in the money he or she earns. However, this opportunity requires that, for the next 2 to 4 years, your spouse will have to spend extra time working and studying. How much "family time" are you willing to sacrifice so that your spouse can take advantage of this opportunity?

a) None
b) 1 to 2 evenings weekly
c) 1 to 2 evenings weekly, plus 1or 2 weekends per month
d) 3 to 4 evenings weekly
e) 3 to 4 evenings weekly, plus 1or 2 weekends per month
f) As much as necessary

D – Relationships

20) How much of the housework should you be responsible for?

a) All b) None c) I should help out only if my spouse is not feeling well d) 50-50 e) Help when I can

21) How often should you have a night out with your friends, apart from your spouse?

a) Never b) Rarely c) Once a week d) Once a month

22) How do you view the relationship between you and your spouse?

a) Two separate individuals who love and depend on each other

b) A team, & I'm the coach
c) A team, & my spouse is the coach
d) A team with no coach
e) Two people living one life

23) For each of the following goals, explain what would you like to see take place (or continue) in your marriage so as to preserve and strengthen the following relationships between you and your spouse.

a) Being "best friends"
b) Being open with each other. Sharing hopes & fears. Knowing and understanding how the other person feels. Having long and enjoyable conversations.
c) Having "fun" times together.
d) Meeting each other's emotional and physical needs.

e) Having useful, loving, and calm discussions about "tough topics" such as finances. "Arguing fairly" when disagreements come up.

f) Sharing each other's interests and activities.

g) Maintaining a loving, equally shared relationship with each other's relatives (your respective in-laws).

h) Avoiding the pitfall of taking each other for granted.

Using the inventory will help you clarify your wishes and expectations. Now you can work towards understanding your spouse's adherence to his or her position. Keeping both points in mind the next step is to work through your collective wish list and look for possible areas of compromise. One way to visualize your areas of compromises is by making two lists: Your wishes that can't be compromised, and your wishes that can be compromised.

Husband		Wife	
Wishes that can not be compromised:	Wishes that can be compromised:	Wishes that can be compromised:	Wishes that can not be compromised:
-	-	-	-
-	-	-	-
-	-	-	-
-	-	-	-
-	-	-	-
	-	-	

With your answers in mind, go ahead and make a third list of the areas that you are both willing to make some compromise about and place them in a circle. Of course there may still be issues beyond immediate compromise. And that's okay. The goal is to show each other some amount of flexibility. By exhibiting a measure of good will you will be sending a message that you are committed to the relationship and are trying to create a win/win environment to the best of your abilities.

Where we are both willing to make some compromise:

-

-

-

-

-

-

Finding some room for compromise - although it may not be perfect - is the best strategy for living your marriage "beyond the moment."

First Aid Relationship Tips

Examine Your Style of Commuication

Seek Win/Win Attitude

Compromise When Possible

CHAPTER 6
HOW YOUR MARRIAGE
AFFECTS YOUR CHILDREN

In This Chapter:

• The effects of parental conflict upon children

• Identifying "Triangling" with children

• How to help your children when the parental relationship is troubled

• Exploring the rewards and challenges of parenthood

When parents come to talk to me about a troubled child or teenager, I often find it helpful to explore whether or not their marriage is causing their teenager to be at risk.

It's no coincidence that difficult marriages create difficult children. Children want their parents to be happy, and they want their parents to be together. When things are going wrong in the parents' relationship, children are often the first to sense that Mommy and Daddy are not getting along. Even if parents say that they are only arguing behind closed doors, children can still sense that something may not be right.

The parents' relationship may be one of the most important factors influencing a teenager's behavior. How parents learn to manage conflicts between themselves can make a difference in their teenagers' lives. Unresolved conflict has a tremendous negative impact. It directly affects the two parents involved, as they carry out their normal duties. And when parents become preoccupied with their own marital discord, teenagers can feel rejected, depressed, and isolated from their parents.

Marital conflict affects teenagers in various ways. First, conflict between the parents tends to both change the mood of household interactions and shifts the parents' attention to the negative behaviors of their children. Second, parental conflict leads to parents issuing confusing and threatening commands to their children. Third, children who are exposed to harsh discipline practices at home (which tend to coincide with a negative and hostile relationship between the parents) are more at risk for aggression, internalizing by withdrawing, and depressive symptoms.

In addition, I have found that when teenagers are exposed to high levels of conflict between their parents, they don't get used to it. They become more sensitive and reactive to it, which causes many of the symptoms of at-risk behavior. Even moderate amounts of parental conflict can wreak havoc on the lives of children, disrupting their sleep and causing negative feelings in their day-to-day lives.

In many instances, parents are unaware that they might be using their children to channeling the anger they feel toward their spouse. This phenomenon, called "triangling," is a very dangerous pattern of behavior that can have serious implications for children and teenagers.

Here is how triangling works. Suppose a wife is angry at her husband for not being affectionate toward her. If she is unable to express her feelings to her husband in a direct way, she may unwittingly begin to use her children to communicate to her husband her feelings of displeasure and anger. For example, she may turn to her daughter in front of her husband and say, "Oh, Daddy seems very tense today and I guess he has no time for the family." In this case, the parent is unable to negotiate her own needs and inappropriately begins to involve her child in a private marital issue.

The child who is caught in a triangle like this has become an inappropriate conduit for the expression of the mother's anger towards her husband. When this happens, children can develop feelings of disillusionment, fear, insecurity, and vulnerability. They also may feel that they have to take sides because they can't manage the internal tension and the anxiety by themselves. In these cases, they may see one parent as mostly bad and the other parent as mostly good. This is damaging to children because it reinforces an attitude by which they view the world in a "black and white," or an "all or nothing" way, rather than with a more balanced view of good and bad in most people.

Here are some of the signs that you are engaged in triangling:

- Do you want your child to talk to or do something to your spouse?

- Do you talk about your spouse to your child only in terms of the other's negative qualities?

- Do you or your wife blame your children for your problems?

- Do your children tell you that they feel anxious around your spouse?

- Do you think your child can bring peace between members of your family?

Parental conflict affects children in varying ways, depending on their age. For example, teenagers around the age of fifteen or sixteen are most likely to involve themselves in their parents' battles. Younger children may keep their feelings hidden inside and may only show signs of depression in late childhood or early adolescence. Other children may adapt to parental fighting by becoming "too good." To stop the fighting, they try to become perfect children. These model children try to do everything right while walking on egg shells, fearing their family will collapse if they make a mistake.

Unfortunately, more and more children seem to be growing up in families with marital conflict: ". . . the number of divorced Americans rose from 4.3 million in 1970 to 18.3 million in 1996, and the trend is so well established that, "40 percent of all children born in the 1970s and 1980s — today's teenagers and young adults — have experienced the breakup of their family through divorce."[2] To this large number, add all the children whose parents are unhappy with each other but who don't divorce. It's not hard to see that a substantial segment of the population grows up in very unhappy homes.

Here are some effects that divorce may have on children and teenagers:

Children whose parents have divorced are increasingly the victims of abuse and neglect. They exhibit more health problems, as well as behavioral and emotional problems, are involved more frequently in crime and drug abuse, and have higher rates of suicide.

Children of divorced parents more frequently demonstrate a diminished learning capacity, performing more poorly than their peers from intact two-parent families in reading, spelling, and math. They also are more likely to repeat a grade and to have higher drop-out rates and lower rates of college graduation.

Divorce generally reduces the income of the child's primary household and seriously diminishes the potential of every member of the household to accumulate wealth. For families that were not poor before the divorce, the drop in income can be as much as 50 percent. Moreover, decline in income is intergenerational, since children whose parents divorce are likely to earn less as adults than children raised in intact families.

Religious worship, which has been linked to health and happiness as well as longer marriages and better family life, is less prevalent in divorced families.

Parents usually experience a lot of pain when divorced, and the most common ways of handling that pain are either to withdraw from their children or to become overprotective. Children are sensitive to their parents' feelings and have many ways of dealing with this trouble, either internally or externally. Children may respond with depression or guilt, that somehow the pain is entirely their fault. Most children have a never-ending hope that their parents will reconcile, even after one or both parents have remarried. Therefore, a sense of abandonment by one or both parents is very common for such children and may contribute to at-risk behavior during adolescence.

Relationship Quiz

Assessing your Marriage

Parents of a teenager at risk need to ask themselves some very pointed questions to evaluate the quality of their marriage. Some of the questions are listed here:

- Are you sensitive to your spouse's needs?

- Do you argue in a fair manner?

- Do you resolve conflicts easily?

- When you talk to each other, do feel you have been heard?

- If not, why not?

- Are you content with your emotional, social and physical intimacy?

- Do you have fun together? Do you joke about the bad times you may be having in a friendly way?

- Are you forgiving with each other?

- How do you handle the division of household responsibilities?

Take a few minutes with your spouse, to evaluate how you are doing in your marriage. The first step you must take is acknowledging and accepting any trouble in your marriage. It is common for people to brush off an issue, expecting it will take care of itself and eventually go away. Nobody wants marital problems, but if you ignore them, you will only be giving them room to grow. Talk to your spouse about problems and work together for a solution with which you both agree and feel comfortable.

Not all marital issues can be resolved by the couple. Some marriage problems are too sensitive to handle alone. The subjects of such problems might include unfaithfulness; sexual frustrations; conflict involving in-laws, friends, siblings, and children; verbal abuse; and so on. When dealing with such problems, the best course is to ask a professional outside party for advice and opinions.

Why You Should Receive Expert Advice

Many people hesitate to receive expert advice because they are unfamiliar with it and feel uncomfortable. But professional advice is helpful and important because relationship experts have studied and dealt with similar or identical situations to yours, and they can assist you in seeing your situation from many perspectives with several solutions, of which one or more will suit you and your marriage best.

Relationship Tips

No matter what your marital trouble may be, always re-member these important steps:

- Acknowledge and accept the problem.

- Ask yourself why the problem troubles you.

- Approach your spouse with your thoughts and feelings.

- Talk it out.

- Stay rational.

- Seek an expert's opinion and advice.

If after evaluating your marriage, you have found unre-solved areas of tension, it's important to try to resolve your problems before they spill over into the life of your child or teen. Improving your marriage may be the most important thing you can do to help your teenager.

Moshe Drops Out of School

A few years ago, a couple, Sarah and Joseph, came to see me about their son, Moshe, 16, who was experiencing extreme difficulty in school. Moshe did not have any serious learning problems. In fact, he was exceptionally bright and capable of succeeding in school. His problem was that he was frequent-ly missing class. Recently he had started leaving school and spending time in an unknown location. Moshe's parents were naturally concerned for his future.

When I first met Sarah and Joseph, I was immediately struck by how unhappy their marriage seemed to be. Joseph was a quiet and reserved man compared to his wife. Sarah seemed extremely worried about whether everything was all right with her son.

When Sarah and Joseph tried to explain to me why they thought Moshe was in trouble, the discussion always seemed to turn into an argument. Joseph believed that his wife's inability to nurture their son was the cause of Moshe's school issues. Sarah, on the other hand, believed that the source of the problem was Joseph's inability to communicate in a warm way with their son.

Here is a dialogue from one of our sessions:

Daniel Schonbuch (DS): Tell me more about the general atmosphere in the house.

Sarah: Well, our family time is not very enjoyable. I would say that Shabbos meals are the most difficult time of our week. To start with, Joseph doesn't run a very nice Shabbos meal. He is so tired from work that when Shabbos rolls around, he goes to shul, makes Kiddush, and then totally withdraws into himself.

DS: Is Shabbos that hard for you?

Joseph: Look, it's not that I don't care about the family; it's just that I feel so burnt out after work. When I come home, the kids are always yelling and I just want some peace and quiet. I guess on Shabbos I just need a break.

Sarah: It's worse than that. You never have time for the kids or for me. When you're home, you just surf on the Internet, and on Shabbos you read the newspaper. Don't you realize that Moshe needs to talk to you?

DS: I guess things are hard during Shabbos. What about your own relationship outside of your children? How well do you get along?

Sarah: To be perfectly honest, we don't have much of a relationship. Joseph isn't very excited about talking to me and we never go on vacation anymore.

Joseph: That's not true. Last Pesach we went away to Florida for the Seder meals.

Sarah: We barely talked the entire week. I think you enjoyed your friends more than you enjoyed the family.

Joseph: What do you want from me? I tried my best. I can't stand when everyone is nagging — your parents, the kids, you.

DS: Have you been having trouble relating for some time?

Sarah: Yes. I would say for about the last three years.

DS: Why? What was going on in your lives three years ago?

Sarah: Well, my husband is in computers, and after 9/11 his company started downscaling and he lost his job.

DS: What did you do?

Joseph: I was on unemployment for about four months when I found a job with another company.

DS: Are you happier now?

Joseph: Not really. It's an average job, and I don't really enjoy the work I am doing. However, it does pay the bills.

DS: That's a big burden, having to support your family doing something you don't enjoy.

Joseph: I wish I could get out of it, but it's not easy to switch at my age.

I realized that at this point I had found a small opening that perhaps would help us to explore their relationship in connection to their son's delinquency. Sarah had mentioned that her husband lost his job about three years ago. I wondered if this also had a significant impact on Moshe.

DS: You mentioned before that the problems at work started about three years before. When did Moshe start having trouble in school?

Sarah: About two years ago.

DS: Is it possible that some of the work stress started spilling over into Moshe's life just after Joseph lost his job?

Sarah: Maybe, but I'm not sure.

DS: Is it possible that the strain on the family became greater after Joseph lost his job, and this is the reason that you also are not getting along so well anymore?

Sarah: It's possible. Two years ago I started working again, and since then I have been unable to give the kids the kind of attention I used to give before things got hard.

During that session, I was able to refocus their energy from solving Moshe's problem to solving their marital discord. Over the next few sessions, we began exploring the way Relationship Theory could help their marriage. We talked about spending quality time together, understanding each other's needs, and reducing critical and destructive language.

After six months of working with this family, I began to see changes in the way they related to their son. Moshe began to feel more comfortable in their home and was more willing to give school a try and focus on his studies.

In general, Moshe's family was typical of the families I see with teens at risk.

Often some type of emotional imbalance exists in the family and eventually one or more children begin to exhibit signs of distress. When such symptoms of distress crop up,, the best approach is to seek out professional advice and find ways to improve the relationship with the teenager.

Resolving conflict between the parents is a positive step parents can take to help support the emotional growth of their children. A good marital or family counselor will be able to break habitual patterns of triangling, and relieve the emotional distress that may be contributing to a teenager's at risk behavior.

First Aid Relationship Tips

 Explore your relationship with your spouse and check for any unresolved issues that may be affecting your teenager.

 Avoid triangling and using your teenager to communicate with your spouse.

 When necessary, seek professional advice on how to improve your marriage.

First Aid Exercise 11: Exploring The Rewards And Challenges Of Parenthood

What impact have children had on your marriage?

How has your marriage changed from life without children to life with children?

In what ways is parenthood the same or different than you expected?

What are your thoughts and feelings about parenthood?

As parenting is a mutual journey of discovery, what do your children learn from you, and what do you learn from them?

What are your hopes for your children?

What legacies will be passed from one generation to the next?

CHAPTER 7
MANAGING MONEY TOGETHER

In This Chapter:

• Learning to manage money together

• Making a monthly budget

• Understanding attitudes about finances and marriage

• Talking about money

You marry for love and friendship. Yet there are practical concerns about how to make a living and how to manage your finances that can affect the quality of your marriage.

Before getting married each person's money comes from their family or from their job. Either way, a couple needs to deal with a new partnership. They will have to deal with questions such as who controls their money, and who has the final say over their finances.

These questions may sound innocuous, but they're not. Money is more than just the paper it is printed on; it's about power, pleasure and utilizing resources in family life.

Some families find financial management easy, while others clearly need some advice. Take Yanki, 29, and Sarah, 28, for example, who came to speak with me about the fight they were having over how they invested money. Sarah began by telling me that Yanki had spent their money without telling her.

A few months into their marriage, Yanki told her about a "safe" business investment, which a friend had mentioned. The business consisted of selling tax-deferred college savings plans on the Internet.

Yanki claimed that they would only have to invest only $2000 to get started, and that they would not have to do too much work to reap results. Sarah was hesitant about taking money out of their savings for something they knew so little about. She told him that she wanted to take some time to think about it and decide later. About a week later, when she was updating their checking account, she came across a receipt that showed that Yanki had paid the investment fee for the business, three days earlier. She was furious and distraught that he would do something when they had agreed to wait.

This is how she described her interaction that night when Yanki came home from work. "My anger built as I waited for him to come home from work. I yelled at him and asked, "How could you go behind my back and spend this money? I thought we were going to discuss this and decide together!" I expected Yanki to apologize or give me a rational explanation. Instead, he clammed up and said, "I won't talk to you about this when you're yelling at me!"

They didn't speak for several days.

From Yanki's perspective, he thought it was a good investment. He felt responsible for their financial future, and was always on the lookout for ways to supplement their income. When a business associate told him about a new home-based business, it sounded like a great idea. He couldn't wait to tell Sarah about it and get involved immediately. But because she was apprehensive, he agreed to wait until they could discuss things further.

But a few days later, while out of town on business, he ran into this business associate again. He warned him that he needed to act immediately if he and Sarah were to benefit from this great deal. The initial investment fee was about to increase by $200, and the deadline to pay the lower fee was that day. Although he'd promised Sarah that he wouldn't act until they talked things through, he didn't want to discuss it over the phone. Not only does Sarah's job as a teacher make it difficult to speak with her during the day, he thought she'd respond better face to face. He was sure she'd want to save $200! He decided that he would explain it to her when he got home two days later. She'd understand once she knew the situation.

Before he could explain, though, she had found the receipt and attacked him. He explained that he was so offended that he didn't want to talk to her until she calmed down.

Eventually they were able to discuss each of their fears, concerns and expectations with me, and I suggested they create a plan for how they'd handle financial decisions from that point on. Any time a major purchase was going to involve removing money from their savings account, they needed to discuss it together before making a final decision. If something came up that would take them outside of their budget, they would need to meet together and decide what would be best for both of them.

As Yanki's and Sarah's story showed, financial planning is important because many family conflicts revolve around acquiring, keeping and spending money. Many people make their lives miserable through constant striving for more and more money and material possessions, in an effort to achieve economic security.

Even if you doubt that you'll be making unexpected investments, all families live under some form of economic pressure and tension. In our community, for example, couples tend to delay their professional careers in order to continue their Torah studies or raise their children. Many will face the following questions: Who opens the charge accounts? Who pays the bills? What kind of bank account will be established? Does one have to ask the other for money? Is one accountable to the other?

It will also help to know each other's values (what is important to your spouse), and to understand his or her attitudes about money. As a couple, you need to discuss how money will be spent, and determine who is responsible for your finances.

For example, in some homes, one person may be responsible for balancing the checkbook, and purchasing items for the house such as appliances and kitchenware. In other families, both husband and wife write checks and actually never keep a record of how much money is coming in and how much is going out. So, when talking about how money is managed, you need to be honest about your feelings. If you resent having to ask the other for money, say so. If you think that the "head of the house" has certain responsibilities, say so. To hide such feelings is far more destructive over time than to reveal them.

First Aid Relationship Tips

Your feelings about money and the value you place on what money can buy will influence the procedures you use for planning and controlling your money. Here are some tips for managing your money:

 Take a financial attitudes test

 Create a monthly budget and stick to it

 Learn to be content with what you have

First Aid Exercise 12: How Do You Relate To Money

To help couples better understand where they stand, here is a short mini quiz that both partners can take and use to facilitate a discussion about money.

1. We talk about money regularly.

- True

- False

2. We have decided who will handle the bills after we marry.

- True

- False

3. I feel my future spouse manages his/her own money well.

- True

- False

4. I would feel comfortable if my future spouse made a purchase of $250 without telling me.

- True

- False

5. I feel my future spouse knows what my retirement dreams are.

- True

6. I know how much debt and savings (including investments) my spouse is bringing into our marriage.

- True

- False

7. Between us, we have more than five credit cards.

- True

- False

8. I know how much my future spouse makes, and what percentage he/she is contributing to our 401 (k) plan at work.

- True

- False

9. I feel my spouse avoids sitting down and talking about money with me.

- True

- False

10. We have the same financial dreams.

- True

- False

11. I feel that my future spouse treats my money as if it's his/her own.

- True

- False

12. I never talked about money with my parents.

- True

- False

13. I know how my future spouse would feel if I wanted to quit my job and start a business.

- True

- False

14. I would feel comfortable living off one salary if either my spouse or I wanted to quit his/her job.

- True

- False

15. When we talk about money, my spouse interrupts me often or dismisses my points of view.

- True

- False

16. I feel my future spouse is stingy.

- True

- False

17. We have a financial plan.

- True

- False

18. We've talked to a financial planner.

- True

- False

Scoring:

Give yourself one point if you answered true to questions 1, 2, 3, 4, 5, 6, 8, 10, 13, 15, 16, and 17, and 1 point if you answered false to 7, 9, 11, 12 and 14.

0 to 6 points:

If you scored very low, around 0 to 6, there seems to be a low level of financial understanding between you. Make sure your future spouse takes this quiz and compare scores. If you see a significant difference in your scores, or if you both answered the same, but had low scores, that means you need major help on this important area of your life together. I suggest speaking to a marriage counselor or an halachik authority, and see if you can work toward a better understanding of each other's perspectives on money.

7 to 12 points

You and your future spouse have a few things to work out, but for the most part, you understand where each is coming from. Maybe you won't see everything the same, but at least you've got enough in common that you can make it work.

13 to 18 points

You seem to see eye-to-eye on most financial issues. There seems to be a lot of similarity in your outlook and attitudes. This shows that you're on the right track. Keep talking, and keep sharing your responsibilities in financial planning. Your sense of responsibility shows that you know that financial planning is important.

Now that you've discussed your attitudes about money, it's helpful to make a financial plan.

Making a Monthly Budget

There's no getting around it: a budget is a requirement for good money management. A budget is simply (1) a tool to increase your consciousness of how and where you spend your money, and (2) a guideline to help you spend your money on the things that are most important to you. Following a budget can create money for savings, where you thought there was none.

Take a few minutes to fill out the following budgeting worksheet:

First Aid Exercise 13: Basic Budgeting Worksheet

Total Monthly Gross Income		$_____
- Taxes, Health Ins. & Other Payroll Deductions	$_____	
- Savings, 401(k), etc.	$_____	
= Total Monthly 'Spendable' Income		$_____

Housing Expenses	**Monthly Payments**
Rent or Mortgage	$_____
Utilities	$_____
Insurance (set $ aside each month if paid annually)	$_____
Repairs (set $ aside for future expenses)	$_____
Taxes (set $ aside if paid annually)	$_____
= Total	**$_____**

Transportation Expenses	
Auto Loan Payment(s)	$_____
Gasoline	$_____
Auto Insurance (set $ aside if paid annually)	$_____
Auto Maintenance & Repairs (set $ aside for future expenses)	$_____
= Total	**$_____**

Debts	
Creditor #1_____	
Balance_____	$_____
Creditor #2_____	
Balance_____	$_____
Creditor #3_____	
Balance_____	$_____
Creditor #4_____	
Balance_____	$_____
(figure more on back if needed)	
= Total	**$_____**

Miscellaneous

(Set $ aside each month for annual expenses.)

	$_____
Tzedakah and Other Charitable Contributions	$_____
Groceries, Lunches, Meals Out	$_____
	$_____
School Tuition/Supplies/Transportation	$_____
Unreimbursed Medical Bills and Copays	$_____
Prescriptions, Non-Prescription Medicines	$_____
	$_____
	$_____
Club Dues (Homeowner's Assoc., Fitness, etc.)	$_____
Newspaper, Magazine Subscriptions	$_____

Clothing	$_____
Haircuts, *Sheitel* Purchase and Maintenance Expenses	$_____
Gifts	$_____
Cash	$_____
Other (continue on back if needed)	$_____
= Total	**$**_____

Monthly Expense Totals

Housing	$_____
Transportation	$_____
Debts	$_____
Miscellaneous	$_____
= Total Expenses	**$**_____

Monthly Surplus or Shortage
(Total Spendable Income *minus* Total Expenses) **$**_____

Now that you've figured out your monthly Income and Expenses, you can start to determine how much you have left over for savings. Simply subtract your monthly expenses from your monthly income to find out how much surplus money you have coming in each month. While you don't need to put aside this exact amount for saving each month, this figure can help give you a rough idea of how much you can afford to save.

If your monthly expenses turn out to be larger than your income, then it may be a good time to figure out ways to reduce your expenses and keep your spending more in line with your income. While many financial experts suggest that your expenses should work out to 60% of your total income, the reality is that for most families and individuals, this is not the case. Try to make this a goal, but don't stress out if you can't reach it right away.

Just because you have a surplus, doesn't mean it's time to rush out and buy the newest iPod. Figuring out your surplus income is the perfect opportunity to initiate a good savings plan.

Keep Good Records

While writing out your budget on a piece of paper once every year or so may seem like the easiest way to go, it is wiser to keep a continuing record of your expenses, income and savings somewhere that is permanent and can be easily updated. While software programs such as "Quicken" can make it easy for you to manage your personal finances on the computer, something as simple as a personal ledger or notebook can be just as effective for keeping tabs of your budget.

Pick a time each month to organize your finances, write down of record of your income and expenses for the month, and update your budget. While you don't need to keep receipts for every single purchase you make, try to at least keep ones from purchases over $20. Keeping good records will allow you to adjust your budget over time to better reflect your financial situation. In general, the more accurate your budget becomes, the easier it will be to manage your money.

The heart of any good financial for your marriage is a comprehensive, thorough and accurate budget. Not only can it help you keep track of where your money goes each month, it can also help let you know how much money you can afford to set aside for a rainy day. You don't have to be an accountant in order to put together a successful budget. All you need is a little time and a desire to be responsible with your finances. But the most important thing to remember is that your budget won't work unless you stick to it.

Learn to be Content

Finally, one of the most important ways to manage money together is to learn the art of contentment. We have already learned that making a budget is a simple way to start saving money. The insights you gain will be helpful, but we often ignore the fact that the best way to save money is not so simple. The best way to save money is to change your thinking, so that you consistently focus on saving instead of spending, and you are content with what you already possess.

To develop the right mindset, be aware of your thoughts about money and possessions. When you catch yourself thinking like a spender ("I must get a new car."), correct yourself by thinking a saver's thought ("Why not wait until I can afford it?"), even if you don't really believe it at first. Eventually, thinking like a saver will become natural, and it will be difficult to remember what it was like to be a spender.

Developing a saver's mindset takes time and discipline, but one attitude that I have found most helpful, toward thinking like a saver, is contentment. Learning to appreciate what you have — however little or much it is — helps you to want less. When you want less, it's easier to spend less. When you are content with what you already have, you can go into a store to buy something you need, and not even be tempted to make an impulse purchase.

Contentment isn't something you can learn by following a certain method, but when you are feeling discontent, you can do a few things to help change your attitude. For one, take some time to make a list of what you have — not just material things, but also non-material things such as friendships and positive personal qualities. You may be surprised by how wealthy you are. Spend some time going through things you have put in storage (or have buried in your closets), and you may find a number of things to fill your current desires.

You can also cultivate contentment when you are shopping by looking at things you are tempted to buy and thinking about similar things you already own. Would the item you want to buy be a significant and materially different addition to your possessions or would it be redundant? Think about the last time you made an impulse buy. Was the satisfaction you received worth the price you paid? If not, why would this item be different? If you still want to make the purchase, consider whether you would you use the item until it wears out or whether you would tire of it quickly. When you start to recognize certain items as providing only temporary satisfaction, you will be less likely to give up money in exchange for them.

Learning to be content with what you have is not an easy process, but it is well worth the effort. Once you have learned contentment, saving will become much easier because you will have little trouble saying "No" to unnecessary expenses. Soon, your savings rate will only rival your level of appreciation for life!

True Contentment

Contentment is not something that's found; it is an attitude. There are many people who seemingly have very little yet feel content. Then there are others who are affluent, who have the best our society has to offer at their disposal. Their houses, cars and clothing are the envy of the community, yet they sometimes still feel unfulfilled.

Most people realize that money can't buy contentment. Contentment, contrary to popular opinion, does not mean being satisfied where you are. Rather, contentment is knowing that Hashem has a plan for your life.

So often we get so involved in the day-to-day activities of earning a living and raising a family that we forget our real purpose in life: to serve Hashem. We discover that our lives are out of balance and we don't know how to bring them back into balance. So, we buy more things or get rid of things in order to bring back the balance. However, nothing seems to work.

In today's society it's not normal to step down. Once a person has attained a certain level of income, spending, and lifestyle, most will go into debt in order to maintain that level. Stepping down to an affordable level is considered failure. Yet, contentment can't be achieved without personal discipline and staying within the lifestyle the Torah has established.

The Torah instructs us that money is a tool to use in accomplishing His plan through us. If we are to find true contentment we must establish some basic guidelines:

1. Establish a reasonable standard of living. It is important to develop a lifestyle based on conviction, not circumstances. On whatever level Hashem has placed you, live within the economic parameters established and supplied by Him.

2. Prioritize. Many people feel discontented—not because they aren't doing well but because others are doing better. Too often we look at what we don't have and become dissatisfied and dis-

contented, rather than thanking Hashem for what we do have and being content with what He has supplied.

3. Develop an attitude of Hakaras Hatov. It is remarkable that in America we could ever think that Hashem has failed us materially. That attitude is possible only when we give in to the tendency to compare ourselves to others. The primary defense against this attitude is to thank Hashem for what we have. Thankfulness is a state of mind, not an accumulation of assets.

Torah Insights

In Tehilim (Psalms) 100 it says, "Serve G-d with joy and contentment." This statement expresses the principle of living with joy and contentment. Dovid Hamelech (King David) was defining the standard of our relationship with G-d. He was referring to the feelings one should have when offering the Todah or Thanksgiving offering. The Thanksgiving offering symbolizes a person's desire to be near to G-d, and that he does not feel that he lacks for anything. This is one reason Psalm 100 was incorporated into our daily morning prayers. Our Rabbis expected that each of us would prepare for our encounter with G-d (Amidah - Shemoneh Esrei) by praising G-d for the opportunities of life, regardless of life's seeming difficulties and inconsistencies. By expressing the contentment and joy contained in the Psalm, which begins with the words, "A song of thanksgiving," our mindset and focus would be proper for addressing G-d.

Being content with one's portion is an age-old Jewish concern. In the book of Proverbs, we read, "A joyful heart makes a cheerful face; A sad heart makes a despondent mood. All the days of a poor person are wretched, but contentment is a feast without end." (Proverbs 15:13 and 15)

To be truly joyful with one's lot in life is wise advice. It is a wonderful way to live, but how easy is it to adopt this attitude? How many of us are truly satisfied with our portion? How do we recognize our own good fortune? All around us, the world advertises the goods and services we all seem to "need." Our world is characterized by material acquisition, and to paraphrase a popular game show, "Who 'wouldn't' want to be a millionaire?"

This is the challenge: balancing what we need and what we want in order to become samayach b'chelko — satisfied with our portion. Happiness does not come through the acquisition of material possessions, nor from the acquisition of skills and knowledge. It comes through being content with what we have.

As we look at the entire picture of managing money together, couples who balance their power structure, budget their finances periodically, and learn the art of contentment, have the greatest chance of sharing a satisfying relationship and living beyond the moment.

First Aid Relationship Tips

 Make a monthly budget

 Be content with what you have

First Aid Exercise 14: Understanding Attitudes About Finances And Marriage

When you were growing up, do you recall your family's viewpoint on money and finances? What effect did it have on you while growing up?

What impact has it had on your marriage?

How can we prevent and/or resolve conflict associated with the handling of money and/or financial matters as a married couple?z

First Aid Exercise 15: Talking About Money

In all marriages, couples have to resolve issues related to attitudes and decisions about money. You may find it helpful to participate in the following exercise and come to a better understanding of how each of you looks at your money matters.

Spouses should answer questions separately, then compare each other's answers, and talk about them. The similarities and differences that turn up can spark a discussion of family money attitudes and practices.

1) If you received $5,000 tax rebate, what would you do with it?

2) If you had to make a major cut in your current spending, what area would you cut first?

3) Do you agree (A) or disagree (D) with the following statements? Circle your response.

A D   I'm basically too tight with money.

A D   My spouse is basically too tight with money.

A D   Equality in family financial decisions is important to me.

A D   I feel good about the way financial decisions are made in my family.

A D   Sometimes I buy things I don't need just because they're on sale.

A D   I believe in enjoying today and letting tomorrow worry about itself.

4) I'd like to see us spend less money on _____,

and see more dollars go for _____.

5) What money problem is the most frequent cause of arguments for us?

6) What was the most sensible thing we have done with money since we were married?

What was the most foolish thing?

7) Do you feel that each of you makes responsible decisions about credit purchases?

8) How satisfied are you with the division of responsibility between the two of you in handling money matters?

CHAPTER 8
RELATING TO YOUR IN-LAWS

In This Chapter:

• Difficulties with in-laws

• Defining borders in your in-law relationships

• Start working together as a team

You may think you said "I do" to just one person on your wedding day, but the reality of married life is that you actually vowed to honor several people. Marriage comes with new challenges; some that you had no idea were waiting for you. Maybe you're lucky enough to adore your in-laws instantly and consistently, but some people hit a few roadblocks on the way.

In our culture, people tend to joke about the classic in-law relationship as being difficult and burdensome. Despite our tendency to speak disparagingly about a mother-in-law who is pushy, controlling and always critical, our in-laws are an important part of marriage and the development of our family.

I'm not denying that in-law relationships are sometimes difficult, if not downright taxing. Yet most of us would like to know more about getting along with our in-laws. It's true that when you marry someone, you marry his or her family, too. That can require a major adjustment in some families, so it may be helpful to review tips like these for getting along with your in-laws. That way, you can avoid or head off serious conflicts before they damage your marriage. As many of us would agree, getting along with your in-laws is almost as important as getting along with your husband or wife.

Take Leah, 27, who had considerable difficulty dealing with her mother-in-law who was constantly criticizing her. She felt that no matter what she did to make her mother-in-law happy, she would make disparaging comments in front of Leah's husband and other people. For example, if Leah would give her daughter some ice cream for dessert, her mother-in-law would say, "Don't you think she has had too much sugar today?" And if Leah decided not give her daughter a treat, her mother in-law would probably say, "Do you really think it is fair not to give her one, when the other kids are having one?" No matter what she did, Leah felt she couldn't win. Instead she chose to be quiet, but that made her feel like she was about to explode.

No one is saying that in-law relationships are easy. In-law problems have existed since the creation of Man. Even the Torah describes conflicts between Yaakov and his father-in-law, Lavan, who accused each other of being swindlers. Of course, marrying two daughters of the same man compounded Jacob's problems! Most of us don't have to deal with that level of trouble today, fortunately. Still, getting along with your in-laws could be one of the toughest relational situations you will ever face!

Married people typically have to deal with a mother-in-law, father-in-law, and any number of sisters- or brothers-in-law, not to mention the in-law grandparents, cousins, aunts, and uncles. Holiday celebrations, special occasion gifts, and family get-togethers can sometimes cause headaches when trying to figure out whom to invite or not invite. Then there's the issue of whether both sides of the family will get along.

Getting along with your in-laws might not be your number one priority after getting married. But over time you probably will come to realize the value of maintaining positive inter-actions with extended family. Your spouse will appreciate the efforts you make to get along with his relatives, and that can only improve your marriage overall. Look for the positive traits in your new family members by marriage, and no one will be disappointed.

The key to in-law relationship is to be respectful while at the same time ensure that your relationship takes priority to theirs.

In truth, although they may be painful at times, remember that you are married to your spouse and not them. Instead of expecting them to be loving and always sensitive to your needs, they may not be able or willing to do so. Only you can control your own behavior and not theirs. You can, however, act respectfully and keep focused on the relationship with your spouse.

Deena, 26 and Yaakov, 27, came to speak with me about the way Deena's mother-in-law never approves of her behaviors. She explained that, "The last time Yaakov and I visited her it happened again. Just trying to be nice and helpful, I washed all the pots and pans after dinner. No sooner had I finished than she (her mother in-law) rewashed them all over again!"

Deena is not a newlywed. She has been married to Yaakov for five years. That whole time, she and Yaakov's mom have silently struggled with being civil to each other. When Yaakov's mom comes to visit, Deena really tries to get the house clean and comfortable for her. But after arriving, her mother-in-law pulls out the cleaning supplies and shines the bathrooms and kitchen. Deena assumes she's doing this because she thinks Deena is a slob and lives in filth.

After the last pots-and-pans fiasco, Deena spilled her frustrations to Yaakov's older sister, Rivkah. "I know your mother hates me and thinks I'm a slob and a bad person. I can't seem to do anything to please her."

Rivkah replied, "Deena, it's not about you. It's about Mom's compulsion to have everything spotless. I grew up with her. I know her. She was like this before you and Yaakov even met. When she rewashes the pots and pans, it's not condemning you. It's simply that she had different — and what most would consider absurd — standards of what is acceptably clean."

While Deena couldn't really forget it and totally let it go, she did begin to look at her mother-in-law in a different light. She began to try to find ways to help that didn't involve meeting her mother-in-law's high standard of cleanliness — like running to the grocery store for milk, or dropping off the dry cleaning and laundry. Deena will probably never have a close relationship with her mother-in-law, but these days they are much more civil to each other.

Chana, 28, and Shlomo, 26, have a similar story to tell. They were married for almost four years and each claimed that the relationship with their in-laws has always been strained, and has placed a lot of pressure on their marriage. The dynamics between Chana and her mother in-law, for example, have never been good. Chana feels that Shlomo's mother is overly critical of how Chana parents her children. She was also upset about her mother-in-law's persistent and nagging comments that Shlomo works too hard. Chana saw them as attacks on her choice to be a stay-at-home mom.

On the other side, Shlomo, who is a quiet bookworm, has great difficulty connecting with his father in-law, who seems to live for sports. When Shlomo and Chana visit his in-laws, Shlomo is especially disturbed to see Chana share her father's sports mania — leaving Shlomo feeling like an outsider.

It's normal to want to be accepted by your in-laws. But feeling that you need to be accepted can bring complications, causing you to be uncomfortable and unnatural around them.

Unrealistic hopes cause problems, too. Many parents are initially overprotective of their own child, or have expectations that no spouse can meet in the beginning.

Often new husbands and wives assume they'll be loved and accepted by in-laws, on the merit of having married the in-laws' child. This may be the case, but it usually takes time to establish trust and respect. Just as it takes time to build other close relationships, gaining acceptance into a family doesn't happen instantly.

After all, you're stepping into a family with a long history of established bonds. Don't be too hard on yourself and expect too much. If your relationship with your own parents is wonderful, the one with your mother- and father-in-law may never measure up. If your relationship with your parents isn't good, you may be too needy and demanding in trying to make up for it.

Refocus Your Perspective

The number one factor in resolving problems of acceptance by in-laws is your spouse's support. As with all close relationships, it's an art to support your spouse without jumping into the fight or feeding his or her discontent.

Let's say that Chana and Shlomo have just returned from an extended visit with his parents. She declares: "I never want to stay with your parents again! Why doesn't your mother like me? She told me that she had you potty trained by age two and that you obeyed her without question."

In this case, Chana is being a little overdramatic and overly sensitive. How can Shlomo support her without reinforcing her exaggeration or condemning his mom?

He could say something like this: "Honey, I'm so sorry that you feel hurt by the things my mom says. But I know you're a terrific mother, and she'll come to see that, too. She also seems to remember me as much more perfect than I was. I can remember plenty of frustration and grief, but it's probably good that she doesn't remember all the tough times. I'll always support you in finding a time to share your feelings with my mom. I really think she likes you and won't be able to help but love you as time goes on."

Or imagine that Shlomo has the complaint, "I don't want to spend more than one day at your parents' house ever again," he says. "I always feel like a third wheel. I know your dad hates the fact that I don't enjoy sports. You and he seem to be in your own little 'sports world.' What am I supposed to do — spend my time helping your mom in the kitchen?"

Chana might respond by reassuring Shlomo along these lines: "I'm so sorry that I haven't been more sensitive to your feelings of being left out during those times. You're right — enjoying sports has been the major thing Dad and I share. I know even Mom has felt a little left out when we obsess about it. Let's see if we can think of ways to connect when we're at my parents' — all of us, including my mom. I know my dad primarily cares about how I'm loved and taken care of, and there's no question about those things in my mind. Please give me a little sign if I forget it next time."

Relationship Tips

For couples like Shlomo and Chana, I suggest that they work on the following points:

1. Work with each other

Remember, you're in this together. Never put your spouse in a situation where he or she has to choose between you and a relative. If you do so, you're putting your spouse in a nearly impossible bind. Instead, try to understand the bond your spouse has with his or her grandparents, parents, and siblings. If possible, try to support that relationship. Even if your spouse has difficult parents, they are his or her parents.

2. Communicate directly

If possible, avoid communicating through a third party. Don't ask your spouse to talk to his sister about something she did that hurt your feelings. Talk to your sister-in-law directly.

If something bothers you, address it as soon as possible. Sometimes it's a genuine problem; other times, it might be a misunderstanding.

3. Set boundaries and limits.

With your spouse, decide what's important and what's not. For example, you want to spend quality time together on the weekend, independent of what your in-laws expect. Or, you may decide that you will not take any loans from your in-laws, period. Some parents, for example, let their children eat anything they want, anytime. Others establish mealtime rituals such as: if you eat a reasonable dinner, then you can have some dessert. Working as a team, you should set your own family values, and then communicate your values to your in-laws.

Putting It All Together

Michael, 29, came to speak to me about the difficulties he was having with his future mother in-law. He began by describing to me the positive feelings he had for his kallah:

Michael: First, let me start by saying that my kallah, Rachel, is a wonderful, beautiful and unique person. We are a perfect match for one another, as we both find strength in being together.

Daniel Schonbuch (DS): Tell me more about your personalities.

Michael: I think our personalities are very different, but they complement each other very well. I'm more dominating. I think I am a dominant Type A. I love to be in control and make decisions. I can be stubborn at times, but my objectivity balances that out most of the time. I think I know when to give in and when not to.

DS: What about Rachel?

Michael: Rachel is very loving and her strength lies in her nurturing, caring personality But, at the same token she has not developed a more decisive personality, which I have developed with more life experience. I make some of the decisions that require my strengths, and she makes those that call upon hers. The rest of our decisions so far have been made together.

DS: It sounds like you complement each other. How are you getting along with your future mother in-law?

Michael: I knew from the beginning that she is a very strong Type A personality, who has a lot of influence over Rachel and the rest of her family. Because of this, her mother feels that she must be involved with every aspect of Rachel's life. This means knowing everything that goes on with us; and because she knows how to work her daughter, Rachel has an extremely difficult time resisting the constant pressure her mother puts on her to know every intricate detail about her life

DS: So, you believe Rachel can't resist her mother's pressure.

Michael: I think so. I am trying to build a family unit and this is extremely difficult to do when her mother continues to have such a negative and overbearing influence on her. Rachel and I have spoken many times on this subject, and each time, I try to guide her to stand up to her mother and say, "No," when she does not agree. I've explained that we cannot build a family for ourselves when her mother has such a major influence on her. We cannot take the chance that the decisions we make in our future are so influenced by what her mother thinks. Rachel has tried, but she cannot seem to overcome this pressure.

DS: How do you get along with your future mother in-law?

Michael: Now, as you can guess, her mother and I often clash with one another. I have had to step up many, many times to fight for us; but I cannot do this forever. I just don't have the strength or willpower to spend a lifetime battling her mother's control.

DS: What do you think Rachel can do?

Michael: I think Rachel needs to step up and start making her own decisions. In fact, they both have to make adjustments and come to the realization that Rachel will no longer be living in her mother's house, and that soon we will be married and we will need the time to build our own family.

DS: It sounds like you've got a great basis for a marriage there — you're very lucky. This is normal to a certain extent, especially if the daughter and mother are close.

Rachel by nature does not seem to be a Type A, so it's believable that her mother would somewhat dominate her in situations. Type As have a tendency to do that. She has followed her lead just like she follows your lead to a certain extent.

I think you need to sit down and talk to Rachel about this. Explain to her that you'd like to set some type of boundaries as far as what's acceptable and what's not acceptable for you, for her to discuss with her mother. Come up with a list of things that might come up, and then the two of you can discuss what's acceptable to both; there may have to be compromise.

Once a person is married, I fully believe that a person should let go of their parents and become one with their spouse. That's impossible to do if one is in the middle. I'd also let your kallah know that you're trying to be proactive in stopping what you feel could be an issue further down the line, that may cause problems.

First Aid Relationship Tips

 Work with each other

 Communicate Directly

 Find Win/Win Solutions

First Aid Exercise 16: In-laws Worksheet

What I appreciate most about your parents is:

What I appreciate most about your attitude toward my parents is:

Three areas where I could be more understanding of your parents are:

Three ways situations where I need your support in dealing with your/my parents are:

ABOUT THE AUTHOR

Rabbi Daniel Schonbuch, MA, is the Executive Director of Shalom Task Force and a noted expert on marriage and commitment who specializes in helping families and couples revitalize their relationships. He is the author of the best-selling parenting book "At Risk - Never Beyond Reach," and a columnist for the Jewish Press. Rabbi Schonbuch is a Certified Alcohol and Substance Abuse Professional – NY State (CASAC) and maintains a private practice in marriage and family counseling. He resides in New York City with his wife and children.

Made in the USA
Lexington, KY
13 August 2010